Singing Bowl Exercises for Personal Harmony

Singing Bowl Exercises
for Personal Harmony

Anneke Huyser

Binkey Kok Publications – Havelte/Holland

First published in 1999 by Binkey Kok Publications BV
© Second printing 2001 by Binkey Kok Publications BV
© Third printing 2002 by Binkey Kok Publications BV
© Fourth printing 2004 by Binkey Kok Publications BV
E-mail: info@binkeykok.com
www.binkeykok.com

Copyright © 1999 Binkey Kok Publications BV, Havelte, Holland

Distributed in the USA by Redwheel/weiser
P.O. Box 612
York Beach, ME 03910-0612

CIP data Royal Library, The Hague
Huyser, Anneke
Singing Bowl Exercises for Personal Harmony
ISBN 90-74597-39-4

Jacket design and layout: Jaap Koning
Photography: Benelux Press, Annelies Schoth, Mathieu Mentink,
Hans Tuinman, Jaap Koning, Ruud Prins (Foton), Hanna ten Zijthof, et al.

Many of the photographs were made available by Hans de Back, a sound therapist in The Hague.

Printed and bound in The Netherlands
by Drukkerij Bariet, Ruinen

Contents

List of Exercises **7**
Foreword **9**
Preface **11**
Acknowledgments **15**

Chapter 1
Sound is Energy. Sound is Color. Sound is Form.
Sound Transforms Form. Sound Can Heal **17**

Chapter 2
Bronze Singing Bowls,
Individual and Unique Instruments **29**

Chapter 3
Metals and Planets **41**

Chapter 4
The Symbolism of the Planets and Colors **55**

Chapter 5
Healing and Transformation **71**

Chapter 6
Practical Uses for Singing Bowls **79**

Bibliography **109**
Discography **111**
About the Author **113**

Exercises

1. Listening to Your Outer World **21**

2. Listening to Your Inner World **23**

3. Listening with Your Intellect **24**

4. Listening with Your Intuition **25**

5. Test for Your Personal Singing Bowl **37**

6. Making Your Bowl Sing **81**

7. Feeling Singing Bowl Vibrations **83**

8. Comparing the Effects of Different Singing Bowl Tones **84**

9. Using Your Voice with Singing Bowls **85**

10. Singing Bowl Self-Massage **91**

11. Combining Singing Bowls with Stories and Poems **104**

12. Group Improvisation **105**

Foreword

Each of us has our own specific methods and techniques for feeling a sense of well-being, but who is familiar with *the sound of well-being?*

Everything in nature consists of vibrations. Sound consists of audible vibrations. You could therefore say that the whole of creation, including humanity, is music in a solid form. It is small wonder that people find it easiest to orient themselves through sound and music. Of all the senses, the ear is the most precise, and never sleeps. The effect of sound is independent of consciousness. The influence of sounds and noise on the body, mind, and soul has been seriously underestimated until recently. The negative side effects of industrial noise and machinery, household equipment, transportation and so on, are becoming more evident in increasing occurrences of irritation, aggression, depression, stress, and physical and emotional pain. Fortunately, in the face of all these developments, or perhaps in response to them, we are becoming more aware of the harmonizing potential of sound, and more of us are using instruments and techniques to achieve harmony between ourselves and our environment.

Sound massage is primarily a process of inner depth, inviting a person listen to him- or herself and bringing him or her into contact with an inner quality of trust. It helps one to regain a sense of self-worth, and promotes processes of physical recovery. The path of surrender and *encounter* leads to an awareness of timelessness, which I call a sense of *here and now*. It is the time and place where all solutions and answers peacefully coexist with the problems and questions filling our reality. If we choose to believe that there are many questions and problems in life, we must also believe that the answers and solutions can be found in *ourselves*. Everyone has the ability to bring peace to the spirit, to enter the silence and to *know*, which is a truly restful oasis in an age overrun by schedules, probability theories, prognoses, future expectations, surveys, and so on. The great benefit of listening to your heart, your soul, your inner self—or whatever you wish to call it—is that you *know*, without any explanations or proof. You draw on wisdom rather than on information that is usually warped with dubious interests, or dressed up and disguised to conceal hidden defects. What would you opt for: dubious information or inner knowledge?

To summarize, you are like a musical instrument: if the instrument is not properly tuned, the skills you have learned will lead to frustration instead of success. Just as a well-tuned instrument caresses the ear, sound massage caresses the body, mind, and soul.

—*Hans de Back*

Preface

the sound in me wants to be heard.
it is being born at a depth
which opens up further and further
where my essence is rooted
in a source of ancient knowledge
where I am in contact
with my deepest Self.
from this source, streams well up
which feed me and others
with clear sounds
with streams of life
ooommm

—Anneke Huyser

Singing bowls, native to the Himalayas and also known as Tibetan bowls, are becoming increasingly well-known in our Western society. However, the origin and original function of these metal bowls—with their fascinating and ethereal sounds and their undeniable influence on the body, mind, and soul—are still surrounded by an aura of mystery. Singing bowls are used as an aid in meditation, as sacrificial vessels, and for eating, yet it seems that few people have reliable information on this subject, and in so far as the people of the Himalayas themselves have any knowledge, they remain silent. In my search for literature on singing bowls in a large bookstore in New Delhi, I was not able to find a single Indian, Tibetan, or Nepalese book on singing bowls, but in Kathmandu, the capital of Nepal, I did come across the book *Singing Bowls,* by Eva Rudy Jansen, in the bookstore opposite my hotel.

Perhaps guessing about and digging into the origin of singing bowls is not very important. They exist and they have found their way to the Western world; we can make use of them and experience their transforming energy; this might be enough to know in our approach to the singing bowl. As instruments with a balanced and harmonious effect on our whole human existence, singing bowls could have a great influence—now and in the future—on our capacity for expanding consciousness, for transformation and healing. The only drawback to the increasing popularity of singing bowls in the West is that they are no longer made with the old, familiar shape and composition. With modern technology, which has also spread to the countries of the Himalayas, the craft of the of the singing bowls' original makers seems to have come to an end. All the original Himalayan bowls that are still in circulation appear to be at least forty-five years old. Occasionally, you'll come across new, factory-made bowls, which are a long way from producing the sound of the old, hand-crafted bowls, because they were cast, rather than beaten and hammered. Although they vibrate for a long time and can "sing," they lack a certain vitality; the spirit which is so characteristic of the old Himalayan bowls is missing. By playing them, you can increase the spirit and fullness of the sound; they have to be intensively played, so that the molecules of the bowls become rearranged in a certain way, just as a new guitar or a new piano has to be "broken in." In fact, this also applies to the old hammered bowls. It is only with use that the sounds are fully realized. In addition, crystal singing bowls were designed a few years ago in the United States. These have particular pitches that affect specific chakras. However, the original metal singing bowls are the only ones with the unique, full, warm, deeply penetrating sounds that affect every part of the body, mind and soul.

I first came across singing bowls when I bought one in 1986 from a backpacker who had brought a number of bowls back from the Far East. The bowl, which produces the most intriguing sound, has a diameter of about 4.5 inches, and I still have it next to my other bowls.

The publication of Jansen's book *Singing Bowls* met a large demand from people who wanted to know more about the history, purchase, use, and effects of singing bowls, and Tibetan and Buddhist ritual instruments such as tingshas, bells, and dorje. Since its

English publication in 1990, the book has been translated into French, English, German and Spanish.

In this book I take you on an exploration of the various ways in which the transforming and healing energies of singing bowls are currently being applied. This is a field that has barely been touched upon, and where everyone is a pioneer: the audience and the singing bowl musicians, the therapist who uses singing bowls and the people receiving treatment, and people such as myself who play singing bowls for personal enjoyment and self-healing. More and more work on the therapeutic uses of sound and singing bowls is being published. Recently, articles are regularly appearing in various newspapers and magazines, by people who work with singing bowls in their own particular field, for example, with the mentally handicapped, patients suffering from cancer, pregnant women, or the terminally ill.

In addition to the many interesting facts related to the whys and wherefores of everything related to singing bowls, I describe the experiences, activities, and procedures of musicians who play singing bowls, individual enthusiasts, singing bowl therapists, and participants in singing bowl concerts, workshops and treatment sessions.

On our journey through the world of singing bowls, we will encounter a number of interesting subjects, including: the diverse symbolism related to the bronze bowls; the metals from which singing bowls are composed; planet tones and their characteristics; the chakras; color correspondences; the internal and external hearing of sounds; feeling sound vibrations; eidetic imagery (seen with the inner eye); the healing and transforming effect of singing bowls.

The experience of sound cannot be learned from a book. Sounds have to be encountered, they have to be felt. To that end, I have provided several exercises, inviting you to explore a wide range of sounds, tones, vibrations, colors and inner sensations.

In addition to therapeutic applications, singing bowls of course have a purely musical aspect as versatile instruments, and the pleasure of playing and listening to them is paramount. Singing bowls can be played in combination with all sorts of instruments, and many musicians use them in their performances and in their recordings, in jazz, hip-hop, film scores, and many forms of world music.

All the activities described in this book can be taken as suggestions, because ultimately you will develop your own methods, which is above all a matter of following your intuition as you practice, learn, and play.

A thorough and scientific study of the experiments, procedures, and possible results is outside the scope of this book. However, I hope that in the near future someone will take on the challenge of exploring this field more thoroughly and publish a good research report on the subject. This is a gigantic but very promising task for a serious researcher. I also hope that my findings, which I have tried to record as an unbiased observer, and with which I have managed to raise a very small corner of a much larger veil, will provide a great deal of useful information for anyone who is interested in the effects and use of singing bowls.

Finally, a brief note of warning. Working with singing bowls can lead to profound changes in a person, both spiritually and physically, but can never serve as medicine or replace medicines for serious physical or psychological disorders. In some cases, there may even be counter-indications, and treatment with singing bowls will not be appropriate. In these cases, it is always necessary to consult a naturopath or doctor before starting to use singing bowls or any alternative treatment.

—Anneke Huyser

Acknowledgments

I would like to thank several people who were a great source of inspiration for me and responded quite spontaneously to my request to say something about their own pioneering experiences, their experiments, making music, and their transforming, healing, and therapeutic work with singing bowls:

Dries Langeveld, an extremely well-read connoisseur of singing bowls from the very beginning, he is also a singing bowl musician who has given me a great deal of information about the origin and use of the bowls;

Rainer Tillmann, a singing bowl musician who gave me a number of practical tips on using singing bowls, and was able to tell me many interesting facts about planet tones and their frequencies;

Hans de Back, a singing bowl musician, teacher, and therapist, who spoke to me at length about his concerts and his practical experience with sound massage and workshops;

Borg Diem Groeneveld, a harmonics vocalist and sound therapist who told me much about the practical aspects of working with sound and sound treatment;

Annemarij Barbas, who generously shared with me her experiences as a workshop participant;

Annema Raven, spiritual poetess, who unselfishly gave me permission to include a number of her poems in this book.

Chapter 1

Sound is Energy.
Sound is Color.
Sound is Form.
Sound Transforms Form.
Sound Can Heal.

Yes, sound is energy, and energy is converted into form and matter. Everything was created from the primal sound, or, you could say: in the beginning was the Word, the Logos, Shabda or Om, the holy first sound, the first movement. This is where we come from, and where we shall return.

Many creation myths indicate that the whole universe—therefore including our planet Earth, and all the living creatures on it—was created from the formless non-being, which was touched by the conscious spirit. This resulted in movement. Movement is vibration, sound, and noise. The non-being comes to life in an infinite spiral of birth, life, death and rebirth. An evolutionary process resulted in the development of humans from simple, single-cell organisms. However, every cell of the human body can lead its own life because it contains all the information about the individual. Every cell is also able to absorb new information or transform it to a different level. This means that every cell has the possibility of transforming awareness and increasing well-being.

The simplest way of communicating with the cells is through vibration. External vibrations cause a sympathetic resonance in the cells. We can perceive waves as sound, movement, color, and form. With electronic equipment, such as a computer, we can make sound waves perceptible to the outer eye. We can also "see" sound by striking a metal plate covered with sand, which can cause the sand to move and settle into mandala-like patterns representing archetypal images. It is also possible, with the inner eye, to experience sound or noise as form and color. When you are listening to music or to singing bowls, when you are singing mantras or resting in the silence of your brain on the border between sleep and consciousness, spontaneous images can appear in your inner eye in the form of mandalas, spirals, or other figures. In fact, sound radiates from and off of you, surrounding you like a mandala, as if you were the proverbial pebble that produces increasingly large concentric waves when dropped into water. Therefore, music is more than a commercial product, a pastime, or art form. Music is a universal force that has been treated with great respect since the dawn of humanity.

The Power of Sound

There are many stories involving the concept that sound can abolish gravity. This hypothesis is often presented in theories about how people in ancient times could move the heavy stone blocks of the Egyptian pyramids or the West European megaliths and place them with a precision down to the last millimeter. Up to now, there has been no proof for this theory, but in his book, *Earth Magic*, Francis Hitching wrote, "There is a well-documented ceremony that still takes place in the village of Shivapur near Poona in central India, where eleven men link arms and dance around a heavy, sacred boulder of stone, chanting the words *quama ali dervish*. After a few minutes of this, they merely touch the stone with their fingertips and it rises, apparently unaided, to shoulder level. Whatever the cause of this, it does not exclusively have to be the villagers who achieve the effect. Many tourists have tried it successfully. The common factors are that it must be exactly eleven people, and they must circle and chant."[1]

The fact that sound waves can have a destructive effect is described in the Old Testament, when Joshua and seven priests, blowing on seven rams' horns, took the city of Jericho.[2] Many of us have heard an airplane go through the sound barrier, with a bang that can make windows shake.

The Indian Sufi mystic, Inayat Khan, was also a great musician and composer. He believed that of all the arts, music in particular should be considered divine, because the structure of music is an exact model of the laws of rhythm and sound that govern the whole universe. For him, music is the holiest of all the art forms, not merely performance or entertainment, and it surpasses religious traditions in being able to elevate the soul. Inayat Khan described a number of effects that can be achieved by music, in particular, the creation of the life stream and the awakening of intuition. In addition, music gives us energy and peacefulness, and it can have a healing effect.

[1] Francis Hitching, *Earth Magic* (New York: William Morrow and Company, 1977) pp. 292-293.
[2] Joshua 6:20. King James Version.

Exercise 1: Listening to Your Outer World

Find a quiet spot outside in a park or the woods, on a pier, or on the beach. Focus your whole attention, listen to the sounds that come to you from the immediate environment.

What different sounds can you distinguish? Are you aware of the rustling of the leaves or the hiss of the surf? What else can you hear? Birds, the hum of insects, a babbling brook? Also, remain open to the sounds coming from farther away—a car driving by, a bicycle bell, a train, a plane, children playing, or a dog barking.

The world is full of sounds, and it is your task to consciously distinguish the various sounds and train your sense of hearing.

Music permeates the whole being. It can slow down or accelerate the circulation, it can stimulate or calm the nervous system, it can provoke passion or instill peace. The closer we remain to nature, the more powerful and magical its effect. However, it is not just any tone, or color, that causes a specific effect; this tone, or color, must be in harmony with us. We change, and so does our need for particular tones or colors.

Primal Sounds and Primal Experiences

Because the cells of living beings—humans, animals, and plants—respond so directly to music and primal sounds, it is possible that changes or transformations occur when these cells start to resonate to certain sounds. This has led to different forms of sound therapy, such as singing mantras, singing harmonics, listening to classical, sacred, or meditational music, healing with the vibrations of tuning forks, the sound of digderidoos, singing bowls, and many other instruments. Many natural societies or so-called primitive communities used, and still use, sound in their shamanic healing practices or dream journeys. They are still familiar with the natural laws that Westerners seem to have virtually forgotten. The Australian aborigines with their didgeridoos have become particularly well known in the West for the transforming effects of their instruments. The bronze Himalayan singing bowls are especially popular here. These instruments have the common feature that they can evoke primal experiences through sound vibrations, probably by summoning, on the inner retina, images of the creation, unleashing a "Big Bang" in the listener, recalling deep and archaic memories as a sort of "return to the source."

After a singing bowls concert, a woman told me, "When I listen to these harmonious sounds, I return to the source of our creation, a place where there is only 'Being,' and where nothing is expected or necessary and everything is allowed. Harmony prevails, and this brings about a profound ecstasy of complete fulfillment, being dissolved in the total atmosphere and at one with the formless god." In our turbulent, commercial age, we feel an irresistible nostalgia for primal experiences, including sounds that establish a link with the Earth, the cosmos, and the deeper essence in ourselves.

In fact, you deal with sound and vibrations day in, day out. The question is whether you are still aware of all these sounds. Hearing is the only sense that you cannot shut off from impressions. There is always sound; you cannot remove yourself from it, though your hearing can become so dulled that you unconsciously allow a lot of sound to wash over you. People in businesses and stores, where there is background music all day long, react differently to sound than those who play their favorite music while enjoying a glass of wine, or refresh themselves by listening to the chirping of birds, the rustling of leaves, a babbling brook, and just enjoying nature. In addition to listening with your ears, your body, and with all your cells, it is important to re-learn to listen like a child. When listening to music, a child does not sit still, but moves spontaneously, dances, claps his hands, or sings along.

Inharmonious sounds or certain kinds of music can make you ill or confused with the atmosphere that they evoke. Music often expresses emotions that have no expression in words, but appeal straight to the heart. And music can reflect a mood, such as fearfulness, desire, joyfulness, sadness, happiness, harmony, revelation, loneliness, or erotic sensuality.

Exercise 2: Listening to Your Inner World

At home, sit down in a quiet place, get as relaxed as possible, and make sure you will not be disturbed for a while. Consciously listen to the sounds that your body makes. You will hear the rhythm of your breathing. Swallow occasionally and hear the clicking sound in your head. Or open and shut your mouth so that you hear the soft popping sounds. From time to time take a deep breath, and then let out your breath, whistling and blowing.

If you are very quiet, you can hear your own pulse in different parts of your body, and sometimes you can actually hear your heart itself beating.

What other sounds can you make with your body? Your vocal cords are not the only parts of your body that produce sound. Just think about whistling, sneezing, belching, and passing gas. Or you can clap you hands, chatter with your teeth, snap your fingers. Allow your body to compose its own music. You are quite an orchestra all by yourself!

Awareness and Spiritual Growth

Become the person you are! Penetrate your essence! In many cases, this means removing all sorts of blocks and obstacles. For this purpose, singing bowls are especially well-suited and their use as aids in achieving well-being of the body, mind and soul is sure to increase in popularity. In a large number of Western countries, singing bowls are now used for healing and treatment, meditation, and transformation, opening the door to personal awareness and spiritual growth. In concerts, with sound meditation, or healing sessions, singing bowls are frequently used in combination with other instruments, such as the marimba, didgeridoo, gong, rain stick, bells, cymbals, wind gong, ocean drum, percussion instruments, as well as the human voice (mantras, singing harmonics).

Exercise 3: Listening with Your Intellect

Play a recording that you like to listen to. It doesn't matter what sort of music it is. Sit or lie down as quietly as possible.

While the music is playing, consciously try to distinguish the various instruments and/or voices. Try to hear the different pitches in the melody, and listen to the rhythm.

Are certain sections louder or softer? You are now using your intellect to analyze the music.

It is essential for modern people to relearn to listen, to train the ear, not only the outer ear, but also the inner ear, which is linked to intuition. If you consciously listen to certain sounds and try to distinguish and analyze them, you will become aware of different perceptions.

However, you could also listen another, relaxed, open way, by allowing the sound to cascade over you like a magical waterfall, without thinking about it, that is, by switching off your intellect.

To allow the sound to permeate you, you can create a state of "waking sleep" in yourself. You can achieve this by doing deep relaxation exercises, or by imagining that you are going to sleep while remaining conscious of the things around you. This state of consciousness is the threshold between daytime and night-time consciousness. You are switching off the normal patterns of thought, entering a light trance state. In fact, this state can be achieved by listening to the harmonious vibrations of singing bowls, which increases relaxation. At that moment, you are more open to impressions and perceptions, and a concert of singing bowls or a sound bath works at every level—physical, emotional, mental, social, and spiritual.

Rhythm, Melody, Harmony, and Timbre

The rhythm of sound is responsible for physical changes, for example, in respiration, heartbeat, and blood pressure. Additionally,

Exercise 4: Listening with Your Intuition

Play the same music you listened to in the previous exercise. Once again, you should be relaxed, seated or lying down, but this time simply allow the sounds to wash over you without consciously listening to any detail, but with the full attention of an open mind. Experience the sounds as a stream flowing over you.

With this exercise, you not only train your outer ear, but also your capacity for inner hearing. You also become aware of sensations and feelings that are stimulated in your body by the musical sounds, so that it can open up to the world of sound and its healing effect. This time you allow your feelings or intuitive nature to speak to you.

rhythm incites all sorts of other sensations and reactions: feeling cold, warmth, or rapid temperature fluctuations, and shivering or perspiration; itchiness in certain places such as in one or several chakras (energy centers in the body); involuntary movements such as dancing, gestures of the arms and hands (mudras), eye movement or grimaces; waves of energy flowing through the body, a feeling of physical discomfort or, conversely, total relaxation. After a sound bath or massage, most people usually feel physically and spiritually stimulated and full of energy.

In so far as this applies to singing bowls, the melody—or, to put it more accurately, the sound composition—can have an influence at the physical, emotional, and mental levels. At the emotional level, you might experience feelings of joy and love, but you might also feel tender and moved. Sometimes a deeply repressed sadness, rage, or hatred may surface, or you might experience a calming, anaesthetizing effect. On the mental, or intellectual level, you might gain clarity or a new understanding of logical connections.

The harmony of musical vibration expressed in certain chords expands consciousness and works at the physical, emotional, mental, social and spiritual levels. At the spiritual level, you could experience a change of consciousness. You might encounter unexpected images that have archaic, primal significance, as if a light within you is switched on, and all sorts of impressions within your intuition are illuminated. You might experience a feeling of ecstasy, surrender, and oneness. It is also possible to have an astral out-of-the-body experience or go on a dream journey while listening to singing bowls. You might come into contact with your Higher Self, your inner voice, a god or goddess, or your spiritual guide.

The timbre, or color, of the sound—the characteristic quality of a particular singing bowl or other instrument—is also important. The timbre determines whether or not you experience a sound vibration as being harmonious.

Healing and Becoming Whole

Anyone who uses singing bowls for healing purposes should keep in mind that many physical and psychological disorders have a chance of being cured only when the sufferer's consciousness changes and he or she wishes to be cured. This means that the ingrained, outworn, and negative thought patterns that the person has about him- or herself must first be converted into new, positive ideas. If someone wishes to be cured at a physical as well as an emotional level, he or she needs to become aware that the deeper cause of the suffering may be found in his or her consciousness—at the mental and spiritual level—alongside the key to change.

The person's desire and intention to change, to be cured, and transformed, is the essential, decisive factor; otherwise, any energy devoted to this will simply be useless. However, the intention of the therapist or musician using the singing bowls is also very important. He or she must have the openness, the will, the love, the intuitive faculties, and the patience to help the other person with this process of awareness and transformation. Many years of experience, a thorough understanding of human nature, and a well-developed analytical ability are also essential. As singing bowls have been known about in the West for only twenty-five years, their use in healing and transformation is still in its infancy. Simply following a number of workshops or courses does not mean that you are a therapist or can give treatment.

A great deal of experimental research will be necessary for a thorough understanding of all the aspects of and applications for healing with singing bowls.

In the center of the
circle
the sound
is born.

—Anneke Huyser

Chapter 2

Bronze Singing Bowls: Individual and Unique Instruments

The golden yellow metal singing bowls from the Himalayas are unique instruments. At first glimpse, they may not look like musical instruments; they would look like a lovely stack of kitchenware, and this is what they are, really, although they also have meditational and ceremonial functions. However, when you start to stir or beat these bowls with different kinds of sticks or beaters, unexpectedly warm, deep, perceptible vibrations are transformed in the surrounding air into full, harmonious sounds, pregnant with a whole orchestra of harmonics. No two bowls have the same pitch, nor do they have any fixed pitch in the sense of the familiar Western scale (C-D-E-F-G-A-B-C). Therefore, it is no easy task to collect an octave of singing bowls. There would be little point in this anyway, because it is precisely the completely individual, uncalibrated pitches of singing bowls—which may sound slightly sharp to our ears when we first hear them—that produce a balanced and harmonious sound. When several singing bowls are played together, the intermingling tones start to resonate, creatively producing the most unexpected and mysterious sounds. Because of their spiritual qualities, these very sounds can touch you at the deepest level of your soul, passing their transforming power to you.

The size and thickness of a bowl determine its pitch. Knowing this, it is not easy to tune the bowl any further if you get the feeling that the tone is just a little bit "off." However, some people do tune their singing bowls by rubbing them with fine sand. Fine-tuning is done by making grooves on the inside of the bowl, and this is really specialist work. You could experiment, but anything you sand away cannot be replaced! Singing bowls that were sanded smooth and thin in their country of origin contain more lower and higher tones than bowls with thicker walls. Nevertheless, as I mentioned earlier, singing bowls that seem to individually produce a rather sharp sound can still sound harmonious when played together, so that it is generally not necessary to tune them.

To find out approximately what notes a singing bowl produces, you can play it with another instrument, such as a recorder, a piano, or a tuning fork, to compare the tones. You can also use a digital tuner, which is a small, battery-powered device, to indicate and calibrate the bowl's musical pitch and range in relation to a scale, so that the tones of the chromatic Western scale (C, C sharp, D, D sharp, E, F, F sharp, G, G sharp, A, A sharp, B) light up on the tuner. A number of tones can light up at the same time—for example, E, A, and B—if you use a wooden beater on the singing bowl. However, the same singing bowl can show E, F, A, and B when you rub the rim, or E and F when you use a felt beater. This demonstrates the importance of the material you use for the beater, and that, in this case, rubbing the bowl produces the most tones, with the related harmonics. However, some bowls produce only one primary tone (for example, C) with the related harmonics. In order to find out whether a singing bowl has a particular planet tone (see Table 4.1 on page 64), a tuning device is actually essential. Practiced musicians and people who have a sense for absolute pitch are usually able to determine the pitch or pitches of a singing bowl simply by listening.

Intuitively Choosing Your Own Singing Bowls

Why would you buy one or several singing bowls? It is often because of the way the particular sound or vibration moves you. As each of us vibrates at a unique frequency, it is certainly possible for you to find a bowl with a frequency that is compatible with your own. On a physical level, the vibrations of a singing bowl resonate with your deepest, core vibration and penetrate your bones, your body fluids, and cells. The more rarefied bodies of your aura—the ethereal, astral, emotional, mental, and spiritual body (see chapter 6)—also receive these vibrations and influence each other. You can feel these vibrations flowing through you in a beneficial way. By using your ear, your body and your intuition, you will be able to find the bowl that is right for you. Begin with asking the person who is selling you the bowl, or a connoisseur of singing bowls, for all the necessary information, but make sure the final choice is all your own. You might ask when, where, and how the bowl was made, and what it is made, as the answers might affect the price of the bowl as well as your own feeling about it. You cannot put together a collection of singing bowls in a single afternoon, but you can build one up over months and years by constantly trying out dif-

Rubbing the bowl produces deeply resonant harmonics.

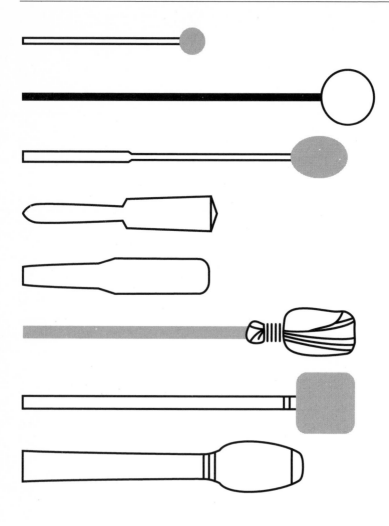

Various beaters for singing bowls: drumsticks with felt or rubber heads and wooden beaters.

ferent bowls, sometimes letting the odd one go, all the while listening to your intuition. Try to prepare yourself in advance for being receptive to the sounds by working on this in your inner self; some of the listening exercises in this book could be helpful for this purpose. When you buy singing bowls, and whenever you want to play them, make sure that you are firmly earthed, with both feet on the ground, and open-minded. If you want to buy a bowl for someone else, try to focus on this person as much as possible, and, again, allow your intuition to decide which bowl to choose. When you are given a bowl as a present, it has usually been chosen with great care, and the intention and emotional message of the giver is interwoven with you in the gift.

The Subtle Interplay of Male and Female Energies

A singing bowl and a beater are not simply objects with which you produce a sound; there is an added value in their symbolic significance. Ted Andrews describes these in his book *Crystal Balls & Crystal Bowls* in terms of male and female energies.

Most people intuitively sense that a singing bowl has a different aura from "ordinary" instruments, such as the piano or recorder. On the one hand, this is because of the mysterious sound they produce; on the other hand, the shape of the bowl is full of primal symbolism. If you explored this aspect in more depth, you would find that a piano or a recorder also have their own symbolism.

In terms of appearance, there are only slight variations in singing bowls. They may vary in diameter, thickness and height, and the edges may also be more like a dish or a shallow bowl. In principle, the shape of the singing bowl is entirely related to female energy. Circles and round shapes, particularly when they are also concave receptacles, represent the divine female principle, the Great Mother, the Holy Grail, the spherical consciousness, the womb of the goddess from which all new life springs. The circle has no beginning and no end, and it is a symbol of the eternal and of infinity. The circle represents the encompassing protection of the womb, where the seed of life grows in darkness, is cherished and awaits the moment of birth. In addition, the circle represents female wisdom and intuition. The Himalayan people's use of singing bowls as dishes for meals as well as sacrificial vessels is reminiscent of the ancient Celts' use of the iron cooking pot or copper cauldron, which were viewed as symbols of fertility, food and abundance, and the transforming forces and constantly renewing female energies of Mother Earth. Ancient cultures that conducted sacrificial ceremonies used bowls of all sorts of materials to collect sacrificial blood.

The beaters that you use with singing bowls represent male energy. The phallic stick represents the principle of God the Father, staff of consciousness, the divine, creative expression, which is essential for fertilization and the creation of new life.

Beating the singing bowl with a simple, staff-shaped, wooden beater produces a fairly short, sharp sound in which the male character resonates. A beater with a rubber or felt head symbolizes the union of the male staff element and the female spherical element, and produces a warm, full sound, an androgynous vibration that resonates for a long time.

When you use these principles as a starting point, you become aware that the singing bowl and the beater form an indivisible unit. Without a beater or similar object, you cannot produce sound with the bowl, and without a bowl, the beater is a dead thing. It is good to realize that when you are using this combination of the singing bowl and the beater, there is something of the creative god or goddess in you. You determine whether a sound is produced. It is in your hands whether or not to create something out of nothing. In fact, they are powerful magical instruments in your hands, representing an equally powerful and magical sexual symbolism which resonates through every layer of life.

The Unio Mystica

As in the ancient stories about the conscious spirit, the word, or the sound penetrating the Void so that life can be revealed, when the male energy of the beater brings the female bowl to life, producing a sound vibration, this is an act of creation. Thus the holy sound, the sacred sound, is created in the singing bowl as the ancient principle of man and woman, sound and silence, yin and yang. This is

Exercise 5: Test for Your Personal Singing Bowl

When you strike a singing bowl with a clenched fist, you hear the lowest possible octave. With a felt beater, the tone is an octave higher, and with a bare wooden beater, another octave higher. You can alternately strike two singing bowls that differ slightly in pitch, and they will start to resonate at the same pitch.

*If you know that a particular singing bowl **does not** have the planet tone corresponding to Saturn (see chapter 4 for greater detail), you can perform the following test to determine whether or not it has a "good" sound: strike the bowl and hold it tipped slightly on its side, in front of your stomach (the solar plexus or third chakra).*

If you feel a quiet vibration in your solar plexus, the bowl is a good one and has the spirit in it. If you feel nothing, or feel a cramped sensation, it is better not to use this bowl.

the Mystical Wedding, the Unification, or the *Unio Mystica,* from which all life sprang and continues eternally in the cycle of birth, life, death, and rebirth.

When you strike the outside of a singing bowl, the female energy vibrating in the bowl wants to expand outward. When you rub the inside, the female energy receives the male force, and this results in the unification of the male and female principles.

When you rub the bowl—producing the fullest, warmest, and optimally harmonic sounds—you can obviously rub to the right or to the left. Rubbing to the right, in a clockwise direction, summons up powerful male energy, which is focused outward and toward the future; this can serve to strengthen your total spiritual and physical welfare because it stimulates and harmonizes your whole aura.

When you rub to the left, in a counterclockwise direction, this evokes a quieter aspect, a female energy that has an introspective effect and can summon up regression to the past. This force has an open quality and is directed inward, allowing you to stand with both feet on the ground so that you are firmly earthed and restored to a peaceful balance.

Tones and Vibrations

The sound waves produced by singing bowls can be subdivided into three primary sounds. An undulating vibration is a sound with a female character, while a short quick, staccato sound has a male quality. When the vibration continues for a long time, the male and female aspects have united, and the sound has become androgynous. Sounds have their own character, color and timbre. Low tones are slow, resonate for a long time, and are bound to the earth; they are often heavy and subdued, and have a full, somber character. High tones sound cheerful, and radiate a lively brightness. They can sound celestial, and have the potential for removing obstacles and old patterns of energy, and for clearing the way to greater awareness, healing, and transformation.

The strength of the tone can also have an influence; for example, soft sounds will evoke tender feelings more readily than one hard strike at the singing bowl. Every bowl "sings" a basic tone—or the combination of a number of basic tones—in various octaves, depending on the material you use to strike the bowl.

Occasionally, tones with a particular frequency can have an unpleasant effect on certain places in the body. For example, Saturn's planet tone (see chapter 4 for greater detail) should under no circumstances be placed on the solar plexus, or the stomach area; no one can tolerate this.

When you begin using newly-purchased singing bowls, it is important to thoroughly experiment with them to examine what they can and can't do, and to become one with the sound. It is only when they have passed these tests and everything feels right, that their vibrations can be used in public.

chalice full of warmth
chalice full of substance
chalice full of tenderness
chalice full of sensuality
when you pour from the chalice
it fills up by itself

—*Annema Raven*

Chapter 3

Metals and Planets

According to various sources, Himalayan singing bowls are made from the seven holy metals—gold, silver, mercury, copper, iron, tin and lead—and the Greek myths link these metals to the following celestial bodies (in respective order): the Sun, the Moon, Mercury, Venus, Mars, Jupiter and Saturn. However, not all bowls are composed of these metals in the same proportions, and not all bowls are made of all seven metals; other bowls contain five or six, or several alloys. In countries such as China, India, Tibet, Bhutan, and Nepal, many metals and minerals are found in the ground, and the traveling smiths forged their products from the locally available ores, which they chose on the basis of their smell, taste, texture, and color. For the most part, the smiths used copper and tin, supplemented with some other local metals—which obviously varied from place to place—producing bronze objects out of these alloys. This selection process yielded a large range of possible compositions, so that every bowl actually became unique in its alloy, size, thickness, shape, and sound.

Until recently, the Far-Eastern countries where the singing bowls were originally made and used were fairly isolated from the West, because of the sheltering Himalayan mountains. However, for centuries, these people and kingdoms have had trade relations among themselves and contacts through marriage, and consequently they had a mutual influence on each other's religion, science and culture.

Religious Ceremonies and Magical Rituals

In the Bronze Age of Ancient China (2500 B.C. - 200 A.D.) there were great developments in metallurgy. The smelting process was accompanied by all sorts of religious ceremonies, magical rituals, and exorcism. The Chinese firmly believed that bronze objects, such as swords and vessels, each possessed a spirit.

It was at that time that the first singing bowls were also produced in the Himalayan countries; rather than being round, they were ovoid, in the shape of a small skull. In the place of the "eye sockets," they had two pointed protuberances, as well as one where the bridge of the nose would be. The pitch between these protuberances differed by a third. The Chinese were interested in astrology, but did not attach any particular significance to the planets, while in ancient India, decisions about important events were made on the basis of the positions of the planets and other heavenly bodies.

The Indian musical form known as the *raga* was referred to in the ancient Vedic scriptures as a reflection of the vibrations caused by the planets and their movements. The notes of the Hindu scale correspond to the planets. Tibetan astrology was developed from these concepts, and it is also used in most of the other Himalayan countries. A mixture of the Chinese, Indian, and ancient shaman influences from the pre-Buddhist Bön religion, among others, Tibetan astrology is still practiced today.

Even so, very little is known about how this astrological knowledge is applied to the metallic composition of singing bowls, or about how they are really used by the Himalayan people. Are they merely cooking pots or just sacrificial vessels? What, then, is the meaning of those impenetrable sounds? Are they used for other, secret rituals in the monasteries, or during these mountain dwellers' ceremonies, which are also inaccessible to Westerners? In the Tibetan Buddhist monasteries, flat, silver-colored bowls known as *gShongs,* filled with jewels or food, are used to placate angry gods. Why are most of the Tibetans who live in the West so silent on the subject of singing bowls? And why do some authors refer to the bowls' connection to the seven holy metals, while others are doubtful about this? When trying to get to the bottom of these questions, it seems that, up to now, we have been abandoned by anthropological research, literature, and traditions.

Mysterious Instruments or Cooking Pots?

In her romanticized book, *Against a Peacock Sky,* the Irish anthropologist Monica Connell describes how she lived for two years in a remote mountain village in Nepal, where she recorded the traditional ceremonies, customs, and daily habits of the villagers. She often mentions the use of bronze vessels for eating, drinking, and cooking. One photograph in the book shows a village woman doing the "washing up." She seems to be rubbing bronze dishes, which look like singing bowls, with sand. Another photograph shows the

Bowing a bowl requires great concentration.

semicircular, traditionally handmade copper drums with skins stretched over them, which produce a demonic sound, as Connell describes elsewhere in the book. In various ceremonies, bronze bowls are used for rice dyed yellow with turmeric, a spice which is also used to place a yellow dot on one's forehead during certain rituals. During one ritual the rice is also thrown into the air as an offering to the gods. Other bronze bowls are used to collect the blood of sacrificial animals. However, nowhere in Connell's book is there any mention of using the bowls as musical instruments.

Other sources describe the role that the bowls have in the mountain dwellers' storytelling, when they gather around the fire on long winter evenings. For these people, there is very little difference between their ordinary, daily life and the sacred aspects of life, so even their kitchen utensils are multifunctional. In order to make the stories more powerful, the storytellers used the bowls to produce sound effects. In this way, the listeners were transported into a light trance, achieving the effect of meditation, so that they could enter the world of the story and it really came to life. In fact, these spontaneous musical performances were part of the sacred experience of the simple peasant population.

For these reasons, singing bowls remain rather mysterious instruments, with their own ancient secrets. Perhaps this mystery will one day be revealed, perhaps never, and perhaps there is no secret at all, and everything that we know is simply all there is.

The fact is that the bowls EXIST, and that we can make use of them. Who knows how much love and care went into making each bowl? Every bowl was made by someone who found and forged the metals and then beat and hammered them with a great deal of devotion to produce a new element containing ancient wisdom.

The mountain dwellers of the Himalayas have many religious and shamanic customs. Therefore it is safe to assume that the latter-day traveling smiths who made singing bowls were intuitively in very close contact with nature, the cosmos, themselves, and their creations, and they actually fused with all these elements and reflected the spiritual strength and essence of the primal sound.

As it is generally customary in shamanic cultures to make ceremonial objects and utensils in accordance with certain rituals, it is also very probable that crafting these bowls for eating, sacrifices, and as singing bowls was also a sacred ritual.

The Metals and the Planets

Singing bowls that consist of the seven holy metals (gold, silver, mercury, copper, iron, tin and lead) are, in a sense, cosmic instruments, because they represent the seven holy planets: the Sun, the Moon, Mercury, Venus, Mars, Jupiter and Saturn. It is actually not very easy to determine exactly which metals comprise any given singing bowl. This can only be done by analyzing a piece of a broken singing bowl, but no one would sacrifice a singing bowl for this purpose.

Historically, there is little evidence, if any, that the inhabitants of the Himalayas had any knowledge of the correspondences between the metals and the planets that is so elementary to students of the Western alchemical tradition. The Himalayan people's current knowledge of the relationship between metals and planets is recent a development and must have been brought to them from the West.

A Female Symbol in a Male World

Even if we do not know exactly what metals a singing bowl contains, this is actually not very important, because the sound vibration and the pitch are obviously the decisive factors for choosing a singing bowl. As it is virtually certain that every singing bowl from the Himalayas contains copper and tin (combined as bronze), with a few other metals in different proportions, the planets Venus (copper) and Jupiter (tin) are always represented in these bowls. This in itself is an exceptional combination because, as we shall see, Venus is a female planet of love, warmth, and art, while Jupiter is a male/female planet of wisdom, spirituality, and the divine in every person. Thus, because of this combination, every singing bowl represents the characteristics of the eternally creative and formative force, the highest divinity, the Great Goddess. If we look at the symbolism of form and composition, the singing bowl becomes a Holy Grail, a womb for healing sounds, a horn of plenty; an inexhaustible source of fertility, food, transformation, and new life.

Singing bowls have come into our consciousness exactly at a time when rational, masculine thinking has reached its high point in our high-tech, Western world. These female bowls suddenly appeared, seemingly from nowhere, from the Earth Mother of the Himalayas where the mountain Annapurna is worshipped as the great goddess of food. Like a plaster on the wound of our excessive and hard, masculine reality, we have been given these sweet and warm-sounding bowls by this great goddess Anna. Like Isis, Hathor, and Mary, Annapurna is often depicted as a goddess with a bowl shaped like a crescent moon on her head.

In addition to the properties of a singing bowl's component metals, it can also have a planet tone as its frequency, which is a vibration that it produces independently from the component metals. Bowls with this feature can be used to perform compositions that have the essence of one or more planets. Taking the trouble to look for the pure planet tones among hundreds of bowls becomes a fascinating search that can take many years. In order to find out which planet tone a singing bowl has, you can use the previously-mentioned digital tuner, which shows the frequencies of the chromatic scale, so that you can see at a glance which planet tone you hear. The frequencies of the planets are shown in the table on page 64.

The Harmony of the Spheres and the Holy Number Seven

Nowadays we think of metal as a raw material for many different utensils or ornaments without attributing any symbolism to them. It is only in homeopathy that we find diluted metals being used for healing. In addition to the necessary minerals, the human body also contains, among other things, the seven metals as basic elements of the organism. The ancient Greeks, including Pythagoras, and later, the German astronomer Johannes Kepler (1571–1630), were already aware that the seven metals are cosmically related to the planets known in antiquity:

gold	Sun
silver	Moon
mercury	Mercury
copper	Venus
iron	Mars
tin	Jupiter
lead	Saturn

Although the Sun and the Moon are obviously not planets, they count as planets in this system. Uranus, Neptune, and Pluto were only discovered, respectively, in the 18th, 19th, and 20th centuries, and therefore did not have a role in the ancient symbolism.

Pythagoras assumed that the whole universe was composed of sound, which he called the "Music of the Spheres," and he developed the theory of the Holy Sound of the primal tones of the planets. Every planet emits a particular frequency which can be indicated in musicology as so many hertz (Hz). In this way the planets are each connected with a certain tone, a particular frequency, and a particular color. Unfortunately, the literature on this subject does not always agree on the tone and the color that goes with each planet; in the context of this book, I use the more empirical premises laid out in the book, *The Cosmic Octave,* by Hans Cousto, supplemented with relevant information from the other sources, including the findings of the singing bowl musician, Rainer Tillmann, whose CD, *The Sounds of Planets/1,* is based on the year tone of the Earth (the Om sound), and on the tones of Saturn, Venus, and the Sun.

In any case, there is plenty of evidence that the holy number seven plays an important role in the principles of the ancient cultures, in natural science, and our present life. The days of the week are related to the seven planets. The rainbow has seven colors and there are seven primary chakras and seven tones. The psychological cycle of human life is based on cycles of seven years, cells are renewed every seven years, and so on.

Gods and Goddesses from Ancient European Mythology

It is not surprising that ancient peoples—as well as people living today in remote parts of the world, where Western mentality and customs have not yet penetrated—devoted a great deal of time and attention to the starry night sky. Together with the Sun and the Moon, the stars and planets provided navigational points of orientation and revealed their secrets to those who studied them, giving us a framework for the general rhythm of life.

At an early stage in history, people had already discovered that the heavenly bodies follow an orbit throughout the year, and that by calculating the laws governing this, it was possible to predict when solar and lunar eclipses would occur, as well as find out which days were favorable for sowing and harvesting, and many of the old pagan feasts (the present Christian festivals derived from these) were based on these dates. The fastest-moving and brightest, most visible planets, together with the Sun and the Moon, provided a whole pantheon of gods and goddesses. They formed the basis of countless mythological stories. Obviously the gods and goddesses were holy beings, and the ancient peoples ascribed a sacred character to these divine planets. The essence, or spirit, of the planet became an archetypal personality.

Because people in the past (and Earth-honoring peoples nowadays) opened themselves to these mythical personalities, the planet gods played an essential role in daily life, and still play this role today. We see this in the days of the week, which have the names of the seven planet gods in a mixture of Norse/Germanic and Roman names. Furthermore, these are the same names of the planets that correspond to the seven holy metals.

Table 3.1 *Correspondences of the Days of the Week, Planets, and Seven Holy Metals*

Day	Planet/God or Goddess	Metal
Sunday	Sun	gold
Monday	Moon	silver
Tuesday	Mars (French: Mardi)/Thing – Tiw	iron
Wednesday	Mercury (French: Mercredi)/Wodan	mercury
Thursday	Jupiter (French: Jeudi)/Donar	tin
Friday	Venus/Freya	copper
Saturday	Saturn	lead

When people noticed that the earthly metals had certain characteristics that appeared to be analogous to the characters of the planets, it was not a big step to attribute divine or cosmic qualities to these metals as well. Modern scientists such as Johannes Kepler, anthroposophists like Rudolf Steiner, and homeopaths like Samuel Hahnemann also made use of the link between the seven planets and the seven metals. In music, Hans Cousto, among others, has intensively studied the relationship between the law of octaves and planets, tones, vibrations, and colors. The vibrations emitted by the planets have an effect on people and on the Earth. Joachim-Ernst Berendt

Ready for a concert...

carried out research into the primal tones, and made a number of recordings of the primal tones of the Earth, the Sun, the Moon, Mars, Venus, Saturn, Jupiter, Mercury, Uranus, Neptune and Pluto, played on a sandawa monochord. The singing bowl musicians Rainer Tillmann and Klaus Wiese each made recordings based on the primal sounds of various planets. In his book *Sieben Metalle*,[3] Wilhelm Pelikan reveals the relationship between the planets, metals, and psychological and physical health. Jaap Huibers describes the relationship between the planets and the homeopathic dilution of metals as a starting point for spiritual and physical equilibrium in his book, *Gezond zijn met metalen*.[4]

Macrocosm and Microcosm

Humanity has always been in close contact with the archaic gods and goddesses, with the spirit of the planets and their characters, which are reflected in each of us through the planets' vibrations to which we are unconsciously tuned, day in, day out.

[3] *Seven Metals.* Not available in English. Translation is mine. **Tr.**
[4] *Being Healthy with Metals.* Not available in English. Translation is mine. **Tr.**

By listening to the planet tones, we can resonate with the Harmony of the Spheres, with the qualities of the planets as they are revealed by the ancient stories of the gods and in modern-day astrology. These qualities resonate in a physical and psychological system, strengthen our personality, and draw out our latent abilities.

The planets are not great figures standing on their own; they influence each other and cannot function without each other. They operate in a kind of closed system, analogous to the structure of the atom and to the functioning of physical, emotional, mental, social, and spiritual systems. The human being is a microcosmic reflection of the macrocosm and vice versa.

In *Planetary Symbolism in the Horoscope*, the astrologer Karen M. Hamaker-Zondag refers to some of the elementary characteristics that the planets reveal in our lives. The Sun, which is actually a star, is the center of consciousness, or ego, and the Moon, which is a satellite of the Earth, is a symbol of the subconscious. The ego and subconscious come to life when they contact each other in an exchange. Mercury has the ability to link the conscious and unconscious aspects of the psyche, and is essential for the progression of consciousness. In addition, Mercury is the neutral mediator that integrates the messages, or psychic aspects, of the other planets. It is no small coincidence that Mercury was known in antiquity as the "Messenger of the Gods." But Mercury also mediates contact between people, for example, through language as a means of communication and expression. In this group formation the planet of love, Venus, meets the need for safety and security, providing an environment for one to develop as an individual with one's own will. In astrology, one's will is symbolized by the planet Mars. One puts oneself in the foreground, distinguishes oneself from others, and adopts an aggressive attitude to anything threatening. The seemingly conflicting aspects of Venus and Mars are to a great extent restored to equilibrium by Jupiter, through religious and ceremonial rituals that symbolize higher spiritual values. With the wealth of experience and by understanding that there is a law of cause and effect, which sometimes leads one to confront painful processes, one achieves the consciousness of Saturn, which is a symbol of the inner awareness of natural law, standards of conduct, and personal responsibility. The newly discovered planets Uranus (metal: zinc; what is not manifest), Neptune (metal: aluminum; the source of consciousness), and Pluto (metal: probably plutonium; dream images, visions) represent the transpersonal processes of achieving consciousness.

> *like a tiny atom*
> *the Sun floats*
> *with her planets*
> *through the greatness*
> *of the universe*
> *according to laws*
> *which suggest*
> *a superior intelligence*
> *as the creator*
> *of this heavenly harmony*

> —*Anneke Huyser*

Chapter 4

Symbolism of the Planets
and Colors

When we look at the characteristics of the planets individually, we can form a better image of their importance and their role in the cosmos and on Earth as a whole, as well as in relation to the metals, the tones, and the colors.

The Sun

The Sun is the center of our solar system and, as such, it is the heart, the center, the focus of our existence, and the psychological symbol of the personality, the deepest essence, the spirit. The Sun is the center of life energy and intuitive wisdom, the divine inner spark of vitality, self-expression, and strength, of the light in yourself and your own truth and clarity. The annual orbit of the Earth around the Sun symbolizes the cycle of birth, life, death and rebirth. In the absence of the Sun's power, life can be joyless, resulting in heart disorders and depression.

The cosmic sound produced by the Sun consists of crackling, roaring, hissing sounds. The Sun represents male energy (yang). The Sun's tone is B sharp (504.88 Hz), the corresponding color is yellowish-green, and the metal is gold.

The Moon

The Moon symbolizes time (the seasons) and movement, joy, and instinctive action. The Moon is seen as the symbol of the soul, and it reflects the Sun's position in relation to the Earth through its different phases:

- New Moon—the Sun and the Moon are aligned, the Moon cannot be seen, and everything in nature is immobile, unresponsive.
- First Quarter—the Moon, seen from the Earth at 90° to the Sun, is waxing; a good time to start something new.
- Full Moon—the Moon completely reflects the light of the Sun; sometimes there is a lunar eclipse at the Full Moon. The Moon is

at its strongest, and it is a time of harvest and celebration.
– Last Quarter—the Moon is waning and is again at 90° in relation to the Sun. This is the time for completion and letting go.

The phases of the Moon also symbolize the cycle of birth, maturity, old age, and death. In addition, the phases of the Moon influence the body fluids, the menstrual cycle, and they are responsible for tidal rhythms.

Moon afflictions are reflected in diseases related to the bodily humours, the female organs, and emotional disturbances. The Moon represents pure female energy (yin). The tone of the Moon (the most important is the tone of the synodic month, from Full Moon to Full Moon) is G sharp (420.84 Hz), the corresponding color is orange and the metal is silver. The tone of the sidereal Moon, B (454.86 Hz), is related to the orbit of the Moon on its own axis; but we shall not deal with this in any further detail here.

Mercury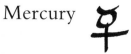

As the messenger of the gods, Mercury represents the intellect, thinking, knowledge and speech. Mercury is a planet for the transfer of information and communication, but also aims to achieve balance and reconcile opposites. Mercury's power over matter is expressed in the qualities of immortality and durability. Mercury-related diseases include stress, migraine, asthma, and epilepsy.

Mercury is a planet with both male and female properties (androgynous). The sound of this planet is mercurial, quick, and bird-like. Mercury's tone is C sharp (282.54 Hz), its color is turquoise and its metal is mercury.

Venus

Venus is the planet of love, beauty, warmth, sensuality, growth in nature, protection, sensation (the Moon governs the emotions), creativity, and art. In Venus, you will find inner peace and rest.

At the physical level, Venus is related to the kidneys, the skin, lymphatic system, the mucus membranes and the female organs. Cramps, throat diseases, and varicose veins are signs of an afflicted Venus. Venus represent female energy (yin). The tone of Venus is A (442.46 Hz), the color is orange-yellow, and the metal is copper.

Mars

Mars is the planet of the will, action, propulsion, sexuality, power, aggression, rage, strength, and enthusiasm. Mars also symbolizes self-assurance, adventure, tension, freedom, and humor—in short, the will to live. Mars is associated with the processes of combustion, and at the physical level this can be expressed in fevers and red rashes.

Mars is, by definition, the male planet (yang). The character of this planet's sound is aggressive and merciless. Mars' tone is D (289.44 Hz), its color is light blue, and its metal is iron.

Jupiter

Jupiter is the largest planet in our solar system and, as such, evokes our higher spiritual values. Jupiter represents universal wisdom, mystical experience, the inner god/goddess, cosmic insight, evolution, growth, and expansion. Fostering development, alertness, and trust, this planet governs our life force and encourages us to grow toward perfection through meditation. On a physical level, Jupiter's influence is related to diseases such as obesity, tumors, diabetes, and liver disease, as well as despair.

The sound of Jupiter is majestic, like that of an organ. Jupiter has a male/female character. In Roman antiquity, he was worshipped as the highest god, together with his female counterpart, Juno. Jupiter's tone is F sharp (367.16 Hz), its color is red, and its corresponding metal is tin.

Saturn

The planet Saturn symbolizes conscience, self-discipline, and a sense of duty. Saturn induces a feeling of isolation and can lead to introversion. In addition, it is the planet that is known for materialism, rigidity, and sorrow. In the darkness of depression you experience being totally alone. You are aware of your limitations and inability, but through this awareness you are able to identify your unique form. This is why Saturn is also identified with Satan, the devil who forces you to see what you prefer to ignore, and it is known as the planet of division and death. Certainly, Saturn plays an important role in the closure of every stage of life. Saturn diseases include rheumatism, gout, allergies, depression, and other chronic complaints.

Saturn's sound is a deep, frightening thunder. Saturn represents male energy (yang). Saturn's tone is D (295.70 Hz), its color is light blue and it corresponding metal is lead.

In addition to these seven ancient, holy planets there are also the "new" planets in our solar system, Uranus, Neptune and Pluto. They also play their own melody among the cosmic spheres and have their own characters. They were discovered, respectively, in the 18th, 19th and 20th centuries, and in this sense they are truly planets of the New Age. They are characterized by their transcendental qualities.

Uranus

Uranus, discovered in 1781, is the planet that symbolizes intuition, sudden inspiration, and the development of the individual on the superconscious level. Thus, Uranus represents the transition to other states of consciousness, as well as variety, independence, and sudden change; through Uranus, the unmanifest has the chance of becoming conscious.

The disorders related to Uranus are often of a psychosomatic nature, such as stress-related nervous ticks and muscle spasms. The tone of Uranus is G sharp (414.72 Hz), the color is orange-red and the metal is zinc.

Neptune

Neptune, discovered in 1846, is related to the highest mystical experience, the transcendence of the ego, and the imagination. Neptune is able to overcome the barriers between the conscious and the unconscious. In addition, it promotes artistic tendencies and religious sentiment, but in the extreme it can contribute to the occurrence of hallucinations, visions, or psychoses. Neptune governs the psychological and neurological processes and plays a large part in physical dissipation.

Neptune's tone is G sharp (422.88 Hz), its color is orange-red and its corresponding metal is aluminum.

Pluto

Pluto was discovered in 1930, and is considered to be, up to now, the last planet in our solar system, though this does not mean it actually is the last planet. There are claims that there are at least two or three more distant planets, which will probably be discovered in the near future.

Pluto announces the beginning and end of a particular stage of life and influences the creative and restorative forces of the body. This concerns, above all, actually reaching your destination, acknowledging the truth, but also having an insight into its relative nature. Some astrologers refer to Pluto as an "elevated" Mars because of the associated instinctive power of will and exercise of power over others. Pluto is also attributed, for example, to megalomania and violence on a large scale.

Pluto's tone is C sharp (280.50 Hz), its color is turquoise and its corresponding metal is still unknown, although some believe that it is plutonium.

Earth

Last but not least, let's look at our own Earth. This is the planet that has the greatest influence on us. It is no small coincidence that Mother Earth is associated with the Great Mother Goddess who gives birth, reproduces, feeds, and then takes back her children. The Earth provides this solid ground under our feet and we can feel rooted in it, so that we are "earthed," or grounded. We are confronted with its energies day in, day out, and experience its orbit around the Sun every year. The Moon clearly has an influence on Earth's various rhythms, for example, on the tides of the oceans, the menstrual cycle, and its influence on sexual and emotional life. The key words for Earth are: firmness, steadiness, survival, solidity, perseverance, and sensory abilities.

The tones of the Earth can be distinguished in the tone of the day, the tone of the year, and the tone of the platonic year. The day tone is G (388.36 Hz), the color is a bright orange-red. The day tone is based on the division of the day into 24 hours. Like the color orange-red, G is very stimulating, has a vitalizing effect, and strengthens the libido. Because of its energizing effect, it is best to use the tone G in the morning, or if you feel rather sleepy but still need to get through something.

The year tone is C sharp (272.20 Hz), the color is turquoise. The year tone is based on the frequency of the Earth's orbit around the Sun (365.242 days) and is therefore also known as the "geocentric Sun tone" (with the Earth serving as the central point), not to be confused with the tone of the Sun (504.88 Hz). The Earth's year tone is the tone that is always present, the primal vibration. In the Indian holy scriptures this tone is known as Sa, Sadha, or Nada and is expressed with the holy sound Om. This sound has a calming effect and is used in meditation; it produces a bright feeling of enlightenment and joy, and can bring you into harmony with universal cosmic vibrations.

The Earth's platonic year tone is F (344.12). The color is reddish-violet. The revolution of the Earth's axis takes approximately 25,920 years, which is the orbit through all the signs of the zodiac. The sound produces a clear mind, joy, and balance.

Tones and Frequencies, Planets, and Colors

Some authors have classified the tones and colors in accordance with the following pattern:

C = red
D = orange
E = yellow
F = green
G = blue
A = indigo
B = violet

However, when looking at additional scientific findings, a different picture emerges. In the first place, the tones that are used in the modern Western chromatic scale deviate from the planets' primal tones. This is because in 1949, a conference in London on tuning determined the frequency of A to be 440 hertz. Venus's tone is A, but its frequency is 442.46 Hz. The color that goes with this frequency is orange-yellow, and not indigo, as shown in the list above. Apparently, several planets can have the same tone and color, although they still have different frequencies.

Hans Cousto, Joachim-Ernst Berendt, and Rainer Tillmann, among others, have studied the frequencies—the number of vibrations per second—at which the planets' tones are transmitted and the frequencies to which our modern Western scale is calibrated. Table 4.1 is based on their findings.

With a digital tuner set to the Western scale, you can strike a singing bowl and determine its tone and what deviation there is from this calibrated scale. Some singing bowls will resonate more or less around a planet tone, but most singing bowls produce an entirely individual, unique frequency. It has already been pointed out that one singing bowl often vibrates several tones. This depends on the combination of the metallic composition of the bowl, its size, thickness, and the implement used to strike the bowl.

Table 4.1. *Planet Tones, the Western Chromatic Scale and Color Correspondences*

Tone	Western Scale	Planet Tones According to Various Octaves		Color
C	261.63 Hz	–		green
C sharp	277.18 Hz	OM (year tone)	272.20 Hz	turquoise
		Pluto	280.50 Hz	turquoise
		Mercury	282.54 Hz	turquoise
D	293.67 Hz	Mars	289.44 Hz	light blue
		Saturn	295.70 Hz	light blue
D sharp	311.13 Hz	–		dark blue
E	329.63 Hz	–		violet
F	349.23 Hz	Platonic year	344.12 Hz	reddish-violet
F sharp	370.00 Hz	Jupiter	367.16 Hz	red
G	392.00 Hz	Earth (day)	388.36 Hz	orange-red
G sharp	415.31 Hz	Uranus	414.72 Hz	orange-red
		Moon (syn)	420.84 Hz	orange
		Neptune	422.88 Hz	orange
A	440.00 Hz	Venus	442.46 Hz	orange-yellow
B	466.16 Hz	Moon (sid)	454.86 Hz	yellow
B sharp	493.88 Hz	Sun	504.88 Hz	yellowish-green

Contact with the Primal Tones of the Planets

In addition to the general symbolism of the planet tones and the resonance that particular tones can achieve at physical, emotional, mental, social, and spiritual levels, there are a number of tones that have fairly specific characteristics, as previously discussed. C sharp is a very calming, peaceful tone that is best played in the evening. It is the meditational tone for singing the primal sound Om and, in many countries in the Far East, the temple bells are tuned to C sharp. In contrast, G has a stimulating effect that can evoke erotic ecstasy. F is a bright tone that enhances insight, helps to process emotions, and therefore brings you to joyfulness. F sharp, as Jupiter's tone, promotes mystical experience and the sense of your own divine essence.

If you want to begin experimenting with the planet tones, you can play singing bowls with the corresponding frequencies, or you can listen to recordings of singing bowls which are based on the planet tones. Do not use these recordings as background music to your activities; only listen to them when you are meditating, because only then can these primal tones really come into their own.

The primal tones of the Earth, Sun, and Moon are the most important, because they are the primary archetypes of our existence, and resonate in our conscious and subconscious, from day to day. However, most people are not aware of these vibrations, and, in their daily lives, simply continue with their normal activities. Nevertheless, these vibrations often do determine the "color" of a day, month, or even longer period. Just think of days when many people feel restless all at the same time, or of the influence that sunspots have, for example, on the thickness of trees' annual rings. Statistically, more children are born on a full moon, and some people are so sensitive to the vibrations of the Moon that they become "moon sick." The primal planet tones can affect our intuitive capacity, bringing up a potential we were not even aware of, and in this way we can achieve transformation.

In order to really make contact with the planets and other heavenly bodies, you can look up at the skies on unclouded days and nights, see the Sun rise and set, follow the Moon as it orbits the Earth and moves through its phases, waxing from the new moon and then waning again. With an annual star guide, you can closely follow—to the day and the hour—the movements of the planets that can be seen with the naked eye: Mercury, Venus, Mars, Jupiter, and Saturn. With an annual astrological pocket diary, you can find out when a particular planet has a stronger effect during a particular period and when its effect is slightly perceptible. You could study what effect happens when you play a particular planet tone at a time when the planet has a strong presence or when it is actually very weak. If you play a singing bowl with the Moon tone during the full moon, or when there is a new moon, what differences do you notice in the vibration and resonance? Is there a difference?

For beginners in this field—and this actually applies to most of us—it is important to start with the Earth tones, G and C sharp. These tones are the most familiar because they are imprinted in us and represent the polarity between activity and rest. The tone of the platonic year, F, adds such a clarity of spirit to this that it can reveal great inner wisdom. Because of the penetrating quality of F, it is best to use it only when you have first absorbed the G and C sharp so that you are firmly "earthed."

B sharp, which is the Sun's tone, can take us out of ourselves so that we can off-load excess psychological ballast and come into contact with our inner source.

The synodic Moon vibrates G sharp, which can be considered a passionate tone, because of its orange color, which is related to body fluids, sexuality, and reproduction.

Ultimately, everything is interrelated, and the other planet tones representing vital aspects of consciousness are also a source of our growth potential. In this respect, a warning is appropriate. Use the sound of singing bowls in general, and the planet tones in particular, with great care. As we still know very little about the therapeutic effect of the various tones and what forces could be unleashed, it is important to be extremely careful. Start with the adage: "When in doubt, say 'NO!'" If a particular tone or a series of tones makes you or the person you are treating feel restless, or become pale and nauseous, stop immediately! Exposure to sound vibrations is not always the correct remedy. If you nevertheless want to use a planet tone for some reason, it is safest to vibrate a C sharp—Om—as a restful factor.

A Rainbow of Colors

We have already seen that in the harmonic theory of the tones, planets and colors, the number seven constantly recurs. All colors consist of white light. If you hold a piece of crystal or a spectrum glass in the sunlight at a particular angle, the light is broken up, producing a rainbow. This phenomenon is also seen in a real rainbow,

Clear, high sounds for the head.

where sunlight is broken up by drops of water or moisture in the atmosphere. The rainbow contains all the seven frequencies that are visible to the eye as colors. In turn, the colors correspond to the seven chakras and indicate the seven stages of consciousness that we can achieve. Chapter 6 contains more detail about the way chakras function in relation to working with singing bowls. The three primary colors—red, yellow and blue—produce the secondary colors: red and yellow make orange; red and blue make violet; yellow and blue make green.

Treatment with singing bowls can often be combined with light and color therapy and with color visualization. Colors can also to reveal themselves on an inner level when you listen to one or more singing bowls. Try to surrender to the sounds and see what happens when you listen to a concert of singing bowls or to a single singing bowl. You may not see colors right away, but after a while, when you are more relaxed, there is a good chance that you will perceive the sound effects in form and/or color. The frequencies of tones and colors are very close, or, more precisely, tone and color are manifestations of the same vibrations, perceived by different senses, respectively, the ear and the eye. Bright sounds correspond to the lively and warm colors red, orange, and yellow, while the more restful and subdued colors, green, blue and violet, are more closely related to full and dark sounds.

Every color has its own psychological and spiritual significance:

— *Red is dynamic, active and male.* The color of blood and the symbol of life energy and passion, red is stimulating and aggressive.

— *Orange is a joyful color that fosters self confidence, energy, and enthusiasm.* Orange is related to sexuality.

— *Yellow radiates from the center and does not tolerate limitation.* This color is the symbol of the Sun. It is warm and brings light and happiness. Yellow promotes the forces of the Self, intuition and wisdom, enlightenment, and redemption.

— *Green is the color of nature's vegetation.* It symbolizes growth, Spring, peace and quiet. It has a calming, healing, and harmonizing effect. Green is the heart color, representing unconditional love and compassion.

— *Blue is the color of the clear sky and deep waters.* Cool, clear, peaceful, blue stimulates psychological independence, inner

strength, creativity, and verbal communication.
–   *Indigo is a deep, dark blue, which is produced by a mixture of all the colors of the spectrum.* This color is on the border of the visible and invisible. Indigo is the symbol of universal consciousness, mysticism, and meditation.

–   *Violet, a mixture of blue and red, is the color of spiritual inspiration and transformation.* Violet symbolizes regal qualities, individuality, and introspection, as well as penance.

> *"Song and music*
> *am I,"*
> *says Joy with a smile,*
> *"sound and color*
> *shape and fragrance*
> *word and deed*
> *movement and dance."*

> —*Annema Raven*

Chapter 5

Healing
and
Transformation

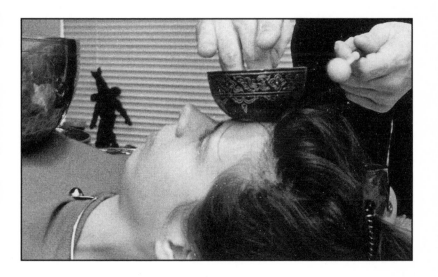

"Wholeness," "healing," "transformation" and "cure" are words that are often used, appropriately or inappropriately, as well as in combination with each other, in modern alternative psychological and physical health care. Many doctors, therapists, and other healers are exploring treatments other than the traditional methods, and in their search, they are finding themselves in a maze of many alternative therapies. Working with sound and singing bowls is included among these alternatives because it falls under the category of "vibrational therapy," which works on the more subtle physical and ethereal energies of the body, mind, and spirit of all living beings.

In addition to the many singing bowl concerts, workshops, and individual healing sessions, there are occasional courses on singing bowls and sound therapy for healers who want to work with this healing modality. Although the use of singing bowls in Far Eastern countries goes back a long way, Westerners are only recently becoming acquainted with these customs, and there has been a rapid increase in knowledge about the healing potential of sound. Nevertheless, this has been going on for only the last twenty to twenty-five years, and it is still at an experimental stage.

Healing with Sound and Singing Bowls

The healing and transforming forces of singing bowls and other exotic instruments such as the didgeridoo and the rain stick are being used more frequently in modern alternative health care and even in traditional health care. Sound therapy in general—singing mantras and harmonics—is also more common. Here and there, doctors and therapists are using singing bowls along with their regular or alternative treatment.

Obviously, certain diseases such as rheumatism or cancer, or even complaints such as headaches or fatigue, cannot be cured with sound therapy or singing bowls alone. Various remedies and countless factors and all contribute to healing, the most important of which is the patient's own desire to be cured. In addition, an attitude of positive interest, compassion, and the intent on the part of the therapist also plays an important role. All these factors contribute to the potential for healing or transformation.

In alternative therapies, such as herbal medicine, homeopathy, and acupuncture, the body is viewed as more than a collection of disparate parts and organs; it is perceived as a complete system in which all the functions and parts are interrelated and codependent. This holistic view requires a responsible, scientific approach, with a large measure of understanding, wisdom, and intuition on the part of the doctors and therapists.

Therapy or Treatment?

The profession of singing bowl therapist is still quite new. Some of these therapists have many years of experience following professional training in psychological and/or physical alternative or traditional health care, supplemented by their own experimental research on sound and singing bowls. Others came into contact with singing bowls through their musical training and experience, and have gone on to explore this area in greater depth.

For people who work with singing bowls but do not have a particular medical background or training in psychology, the title of "therapist" would perhaps be an overstatement, and it would be more appropriate to refer to their work as "singing bowl treatments." Someone who treats clients with singing bowls will not, in general, describe this "treatment" as medical, but as a way of using transforming energies to establish or restore the client's harmony, so that he or she can become whole, or achieve a different state of consciousness; in other words, it's a way of creating the possibility to regain and maintain the person's original sense of well-being.

Disorders and physical or psychological complaints are often caused by trauma experienced in the past. The residual fear caused by such experiences can lead to disturbances or blocks, so that life energy cannot flow freely. A singing bowl practitioner tries to restore energy balance with his or her own methods. He or she will usually describe the "treatment" as a singing bowl concert, massage, bath, or some other term of his or her own. In addition, the practitioner might use other instruments or vocalizations during the sound treatment. There are no "ready-made recipes" of sound that work for everyone, apart from a few universally applicable natural

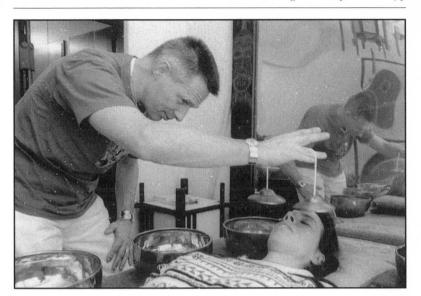

Subtle interaction between the therapist and the client.

and musical laws of sound. Everyone vibrates at his or her own unique level, and therefore there is an equivalent number of possible sound treatments. People usually indicate which sounds they feel as pleasant, healing, and effective for themselves.

Becoming Whole and Healing

Healing could be described as the removal of complaints caused by physical and psychological diseases. Up to now, healing in traditional Western medicine has been aimed primarily at combating symptoms, but in the holistic vision of alternative medicine, in which a person is treated as an indivisible unit comprising the body, soul, and mind, the concept of healing could be described as increasing a person's general well-being. In this sense, the terms "becoming whole" and "transformation" are used in conjunction with "healing" in the alternative health field. Being whole or healing means restoring one's energy balance and innate harmony at the physical, emotional, mental, social, and spiritual levels, and this is an ongoing process.

Katarina van Dijk-Karanika gives the following definition of the process of healing in her article in the magazine *Bres:*[5]

– Consciousness and restoration of the contact between the body and the emotions (physical and emotional dimension).
– Consciousness and adjustment of ideas about oneself and one's worldview (mental dimension).
– Consciousness and development of communication with oneself and the environment (social dimension).
– Making contact with intuitive abilities and creativity (spiritual dimension).
– Giving meaning to one's own life process (spiritual dimension).

Becoming whole is a process in which people consciously engage themselves. In this process, the person who is treating you cannot provide a cure or promise that you will be healed, but can help in his or her own way to support you, for example, by removing blocked emotions or showing the way to possibilities for spiritual transformation. A physical disorder or psychological imbalance is often the signal that something is not right in the trinity of the body, mind, and soul; the balance has been disrupted in some way, causing smaller or greater discomforts that indicate illness. Treating each separate symptom with different medicines is considered quite unacceptable in alternative medical theory, which states that everything is interrelated, and it is better to treat the body as a whole that is more than the sum of its parts. We see this in acupuncture and homeopathy, and it is also the foundation for sound therapy with singing bowls as well as other instruments.

Occasionally, singing bowl therapists are told that their clients experience relief, after only one session, from insomnia, backache, or speech problems. However, these sorts of "miraculous" cures should be seen as relative to that specific person's situation at that time. It does not mean that everyone will experience immediate relief.

In addition to healing, the transformation process includes the

---

[5] This is a Dutch periodical, not available in English. See bibliography.

practice of meditation, a bridge for personal, spiritual growth. Concentration and silence is an essential element in meditation. The "correct" meaning and practice of meditation is an inexhaustible subject. In the context of this book, meditation is defined as being completely here and now, being present in your own center with loving attention, and letting go of disturbing thoughts so that a healing and transforming silence can be admitted and experienced.

In the silence the sound is born
of a sound which wells up
from intangible depths
from my own Self
inaudible but clearly
heard in the openness
of silence

—*Anneke Huyser*

Chapter 6

Practical Uses
for Singing Bowls

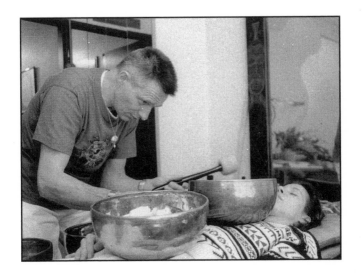

When you are playing singing bowls there are several important factors to consider. First of all, you should be attracted to the shape and appearance of the bowl. Then, experiment with striking or rubbing several kinds of bowls with different types of beaters:

– A wooden beater or stick, which may be covered with a strip of leather or suede, or wrapped with broad, plastic tape;
– Beaters or drumsticks with felt or rubber ball tips in various sizes;
– Other materials that you experiment with yourself.

Larger bowls sometimes have a thick rim that bends in. These bowls produce a sound that moves inward and down. Bowls with a straight edge make a sound that is outward-moving. Some bowls sound very bright, and are therefore suitable for use in more mentally active

---

Exercise 6: Making Your Bowl Sing

Place the singing bowl on a little cushion, a ring, on the flat of your hand, or the tips of your fingers. Make sure that there is as little contact as possible with any other resonating material, so that the air is free to vibrate all around. Also, check out the acoustics of the space, especially if you are planning to give concerts or treatments there. Tap the singing bowl in various places with a beater: on the rim, on the rounded outer surface, and on the inside. Hold the beater loosely between your fingers and swing it freely against the bowl. This creates a full, long-lasting sound.

To make the bowl sing, you use a wooden beater covered with leather or wrapped with plastic tape; rub around the edge, on the inside or outside. By rubbing the bowl you produce a spiral of energy with many harmonics. Listen to the differences in sound coming from the inside and outside and the implement you used for the beater.

No two singing bowls sound the same. Some bowls sound flat or bright, and some bowls combine several tones. If you allow the bowl to move a little in your hand, you will notice that the vibration becomes fuller and more expansive.

OM...

moments, for example, when reading. By opening and closing your mouth next to the rim of the bowl while it is singing, you can hear one, two, or even three harmonics in some bowls. A versatile bowl with three or more harmonics is less common. Make sure that you make too little sound rather than too much; a surfeit of sound or excessive volume has a very restless effect.

Sets of several different bowls can be compiled in different ways:
– as a scale;
– as chords;
– according to the planet tones;
– intuitively, in accordance with what sounds harmonious to you.

Exercise 7: Feeling Singing Bowl Vibrations

It is an exciting experience to learn to listen with your body! Place a singing bowl on the palm of your hand and strike the bowl. Can you feel the vibrations in your hand and arm? After you have struck the bowl, put the beater aside, hold your other hand above the bowl and feel the vibrations. Strike the bowl again and place your hand on the rim. The sound and the vibration stop. Now hold your hand above the quiet bowl and feel the difference. If necessary, repeat this a number of times, so you can clearly feel the difference.

Most people tend to intuitively collect a set of bowls that just sound good to them, and singing bowls with completely individual and unique sounds are most suitable for this. In the other cases listed above, you need a tuning device to find bowls with the desired pitches.

Learning to Listen to Sounds with Your Entire Being

Because of the constant cacophony that we generally endure on an ordinary work day, and even in the evening when we zap through TV channels with our remote controls, many of us tend to become numb to more subtle sounds.

Listening to singing bowls requires an open and attentive attitude, not so much to analyze the sounds but to be present, aware, and alert, and to try and catch the individual sounds and harmonics with the ear. Therefore, make sure that you cannot be interrupted or disturbed during your singing bowl sessions. You can simply practice, but if you really want to listen in a completely relaxed way and feel the sounds, you can ask someone else to strike the bowls for you, or you can listen to a CD of singing bowl music. When the sound dies away, you can learn to hear the tone for even longer with your inner ear.

The harmonics, which are especially noticeable when you rub the outside of the singing bowl, have a great influence on the cells of

Exercise 8: Comparing the Effects of Different Singing Bowl Tones

This exercise requires a partner. Lie down on your back, fully relax, and ask your partner to strike a tone, alternately using several bowls and different types of beaters. Try to feel the difference between striking and rubbing the bowl.

What sort of perceptions arise in your body and in your cells with a particular singing bowl? What is the effect of different pitches, harmonics and timbres? Can you feel any itching, tickling feelings, or goosebumps, shivering, involuntary sensations of movement, heat or cold? Does your energy level or your consciousness change in any way?

the body and ensure that the body, mind, and soul are in harmony at this level. Practice makes perfect, but in this case you learn to listen to your body in a more conscious way, and then your whole body will open up to the dimensions of your true essence.

Resonating with Singing Bowls

If you strike two or more singing bowls one after the other, the resonance of their individual harmonics will produce a harmony. Some bowls will reinforce each other's volume, while others will reduce each other's volume. In some cases, one bowl can take over the other's sound or pitch so that the harmonics produce the characteristic singing sound. To our Western ears, this does not always sound very harmonious, because the natural vibration intervals in the harmonics that occur in singing bowls are not common in the Western scale to which we are accustomed. Therefore, we have to learn to listen again, learn to distinguish sounds and harmonics, and then regroup them in our brain to accept them as harmonious sounds. It is precisely by allowing the sounds to enter into you, and to surrender to this sound that you achieve a state of peace and acceptance so that you can become one with these vibrations.

Exercise 9: Using Your Voice with Singing Bowls

Humming along with the sound of a singing bowl can be a very special experience, because it increases the resonance in your head; your own skull works as a natural sound box.

The effect can be very harmonious, especially if you do this with a tone that you find pleasant. You usually hum with your mouth closed, but if you form the vowels a, e, i, o, and u (or choose your own sounds such as wow, ow, or the primal sound Om), with your mouth open next to the rim of the vibrating bowl—first without making a sound, and then adding the sound of your vocal cords—the harmonics will resonate deep in your head.

Finding Your Basic Tone

When I do Exercise 9 with one of my singing bowls, not only do I experience the amplified resonating effect, but I hear an unearthly echo in my head, and all around my ears. It just so happens that the tone of this singing bowl—G—corresponds to what I currently recognize as my own basic tone. When I spontaneously hum a note or recite the primal sound Om without using any singing bowls or instruments, it usually proves to be the note G. When I acquired this singing bowl, I had a sense of recognition: "This is my bowl, my basic tone, my primal sound!" This sound vibration literally penetrated the very marrow of my bones, which was, in this case, a very pleasant sensation. I have noticed that with this sound I can reach my own core, the center in which I live and work.

You can find your own basic tone by regularly starting to hum spontaneously, and then checking this tone with a tuning device, a piano, recorder, or other instrument. If it is often the same tone, you can assume this is your basic tone, although this can vary at different stages of your life and in different circumstances. It is a fortunate fact that the basic tone of your own voice is the source of your own healing. Your basic tone is your own primal frequency, your most authentic part, converted into vibrations. It is the music which you always have in you and with you, and the harmony is completely in accordance with your existence. Singing your basic tone works like a generator, charging you with balanced energy that you can also radiate to other people. If you think you have discovered your basic tone, the next task is to find an appropriate singing bowl.

Sound Baths, Sound Massage, or Sound Treatment with Singing Bowls

There are no clearly-defined rules for a sound bath, sound massage, or sound treatment. Everyone has his or her own way of performing a treatment, but there are some general starting points that most people use. The typical description of a sound massage produces a very general picture in which all sorts of individual procedures are possible. Some people give one-session treatments or a program of several sessions. In addition to treatments for individuals, it is possible to conduct or participate in group sessions or workshops. Some practitioners like to begin with talking to their client about what to expect, what the client wants, as well as assess their psychological state, although this is obviously not done on the basis of a single meeting. Afterward, they might discuss the experience so that the therapist has some feedback about the effects. Others consciously do not talk before or after the treatment, and see the sound massage as a non-verbal event in which the experience is offered and the client is seen as a person responsible for his or her own responses. They think that it is important to arrest the intellect and give the imagination the opportunity to express itself. The sound vibrations of the bowl open up your feeling nature and give your ego the chance to "go for a walk," so that it leaves you undisturbed for a moment. It sometimes happens that someone who is very stressed-out falls asleep during a sound bath. Falling asleep is okay because it can work as a sort of safety valve, momentarily switching off the rational mind and thought processes, so the treatment can flow directly and uncensored to your feelings, where no labels are attached and where there is space for your own inner wisdom.

During the treatment, the therapist needs to keep an eye on the client and observe the signals from the client's body. Someone who is lying there in a relaxed way with a smile on his face is simply open to the sounds. However, if the client becomes pale and holds his breath, it may be advisable to start with a few breathing and relaxation exercises, or to work up the body with singing bowls that produce a low sound, to create the required relaxation. If necessary, the treatment must be temporarily halted. For people who are "in their head," the low sounds are sometimes threatening: they may feel unsafe with the tones of a large Chinese temple gong, but in practice it seems that the vibrations of the gong are often so intense that this resistance automatically disappears after a while and is replaced by wonder and awe. On the other hand, serious or depressed people will probably benefit from high, clear sounds; this is because their blocked spiritual side needs vitality and clarity. In general, higher and bright sounds usually open the upper body and thus evoke the power of light and spirituality, while the lower, dark sounds influence the lower part of the body with their restful, earthing effect.

In general, you can be restored to balance by a sound massage; old patterns of behavior that are difficult or cause problems are revised, because the sound vibrations break up all the old associations. From this chaos the blueprint of your true Self can emerge in the form of a well-disciplined intelligence that will show you your blind spots so that old wounds have a chance to heal. The entire process is like separating wheat from chaff, or panning for gold.

A sound therapist, or someone giving treatment, needs to have the necessary integrity to deal with people at this level of deep feelings; he or she must guide the person lovingly and with the necessary reserve to help restore the person's sense of self-worth and inner strength, and if necessary, advise the person to seek another form of therapy. The intensity with which the person giving the treatment approaches clients is extremely important and will determine whether or not the treatment goes well.

Most people who give singing bowl treatments and most therapists will use several other instruments, in addition to different singing bowls, including drums, gongs, ocean drums, djembes, ting-shas (small cymbals), wind gongs, rain sticks, bells, didgeridoos, marimbas, as well as the voice (for singing mantras or harmonics). An ocean drum is a large tambourine filled with small pellets that imitates the sound of surf, and like a rain stick, which imitates the sound of a down-pour, it has a cleansing and grounding effect.

What Happens During a Sound Bath, Massage, or Treatment

The person to be treated lies on the ground or on a table used especially for this purpose. All the singing bowls and gongs have been placed around the treatment area in advance, particularly the large ones that produce deep sounds; these can be placed near the feet, and small, bright, Japanese bowls and tingshas can be placed at the head. The practitioner strikes them struck alternately, very softly. He or she also strikes a singing bowl and holds it just above the client's body, passing it from the feet to the head. Differences in sound may be heard if the bowl passes an area where there is a problem. At that spot the practitioner strikes the same singing bowl again. The problem area consumes the particular spectrum of tones being offered so that the singing bowl's high, medium, or low tones audibly sound different. When the problem area has been saturated, the singing bowl will regain its "normal" and complete range. This process is comparable to pouring water on a sponge. The sponge will absorb water until it is saturated. Full is full. This does not mean that the area is physically cured, but that it has absorbed the nectar of the sound vibrations—which provide the best orientation at that time—and that the balance there has been restored, and the area is once again in equilibrium.

Next, the practitioner strikes the bowls all around the body, and gives the feet (with a cushion under the ankles) a sound treatment by gently touching the vibrating bowl against the top and the bottom of the foot, massaging the reflex zones with sound vibrations. Sometimes the practitioner will place a singing bowl on the client's stomach. If the bowl has been rubbed, the low harmonics will produce a constant vibration in the stomach cavity, where there is often

The healing power of sound massage.

an area of disturbance (cramp, fear); this can also gently dislodge small remnants of food that have accumulated in the intestines so they can be passed out of the body.

When the client lies on his or her stomach, the practitioner can place a bowl with thick walls, which produces a deep sound, in the middle of the back. A bowl that produces a bright sound can be placed on the upper part of the back. The two bowls are struck alternately. By passing the high bright sounds of tingshas softly over the whole body, any physical energy that has become blocked can start to flow again, as though the locks are opened. Tingshas are also used to start and conclude a session because they have a grounding effect. Gongs and drums are used to appeal to the imagination and the power of association. Gongs can evoke an archaic timelessness as a return to a silence where space and time have been abolished.

Some therapists conclude the singing bowl treatment by giving the client a neck massage. At the end of every session, the person being treated must be grounded again with an earthing exercise, particular sounds, or suggestive words, so that he or she has completely returned to the here and now and can go back home and to daily life with both feet firmly on the ground. A sound bath can take 60 to 75 minutes, but longer massages are also possible (up to 2 1/2 hours), and several other applications can also be used such as:

– synchronizing the left and right half of the brain;
– breathing exercises;
– the "lemniscate" treatment (a polarity massage in which a singing bowl is moved over the body in a figure-eight to restore the body's energy balance);
– extensive aura healing and chakra treatment;
– a guided meditation/visualization exercise;
  a facial massage in which the vibrating singing bowl is held in front of and against the face;
– more extensive treatment with gongs.

Exercise 10 describes how to give yourself a sound massage. Obviously you cannot relax completely during this exercise, because you have to strike the bowls yourself. You can solve this problem by putting on a recording of singing bowl music. Then you can com-

Exercise 10: Singing Bowl Self-Massage

You can also give yourself a simple sound massage. Make sure that you will not be disturbed. Lie down on your back, breathe deeply three times, and try to be as relaxed as possible. Place a bowl with a deep sound on your stomach, in the middle of your body, approximately two fingers below your navel, at the point known in Japanese Zen Buddhism as the Hara point. Breathe quietly from the stomach. Strike the bowl with a felt beater and feel the vibrations pass through your body.

Then you can experiment with the bowls on various other points, for example, at the chakra points. The lower tones usually work better for the lower chakras, while the higher tones are good for the upper body chakras. Remain lying down for a while, enjoying the sounds and the vibrations you have felt. Then return to the here and now.

pletely surrender to the sound. It is a good idea to first read any instructions that are enclosed with the recording. Usually it is better to listen through speakers rather than with headphones.

As you do this, you develop your own preferences for different sounds. Even a bowl that may sound "inharmonious" to others can be very pleasing to you. One workshop participant said, "I really enjoyed a bowl that made a very high sound that other people found dreadful. I did not leave my body, but my crown opened and everything became light."

After a sound bath or sound massage you often feel more serene, or, as another workshop participant remarked, "When the sound has finished vibrating, the silence touches my own silence and I feel completely calm." Allow this silence to continue for a while before returning to your full and busy life right away. Use the silence in yourself to reflect on yourself and how you can carry this mood through your daily life, to living and working in this relaxed manner, with both feet firmly on the ground. Some people keep a diary in which they record the feelings, perceptions, primal images, colors, shapes, and ideas that come to them during sound massages and workshops, so that they can follow the process and any resulting changes they have experienced.

Synchronization of the
Left and Right Hemispheres of the Brain

For most adults, the left half of the brain is the most active. This hemisphere deals with logical thinking, mathematics, and analysis, and the speech center is also located in this half of the brain. The right hemisphere handles feelings, visual perceptions, dreams, creativity, music, sexuality, intuition and spirituality. Right-brain characteristics are still undervalued in our society, compared with the logical thought processes of the left brain. Children under the age of five are still permitted to be creative, playful, and emotional, but afterward it is time to stop having fun and people are expected to submit to logical thought processes. As a result, many adults are no longer used to using the right half of their brain, which results in creative blocks and inhibited feelings.

Ideally, the two halves of the brain are in harmony with each other. Many alternative methods, including singing bowl therapy, aim to stimulate the underdeveloped right brain so that balance can be restored. Only people with serious emotional problems and/or psychotic tendencies would be helped by left brain stimulation, which leads their often over-burdened right brain out of the chaotic world of feelings back onto a manageable course.

Alpha, Beta, Theta, and Delta Brain Waves

The two halves of the brain—often independently of each other—both produce brain waves, which are all related to particular states of consciousness.

– *The Beta Waves (between 13 and 30 hertz)*. These occur during normal daily consciousness with an emphasis on activity, intense attention, logical reasoning, and "running in the rat race." In our modern society, most people produce these beta waves on a daily basis, especially with the left half of the brain.

– *The Alpha Waves (between 8 and 13 hertz)*. These occur during normal daily consciousness with the emphasis on concentration, being relaxed, calm, satisfied, creative, and loving. Alpha waves occur during periods of rest, relaxation, and meditation. A ratio of alpha waves with about 10-30% beta waves is desirable for normal activity.

– *The Theta Waves (between 4 and 7 hertz)*. These occur during the state of somnolence, between waking and sleeping, and light sleep. These brain waves are produced with deep relaxation, day dreams, the imagination, visualization, staring, and an average hypnotic trance, and they are responsible for seeing inner, eidetic images, memory regression, and photographic memory.

– *The Delta Waves (less than 4 hertz)*. These occur during dreamless sleep. These brain waves can be helpful in recalling hypnotic regressions of the early years, a person's own birth and the prenatal period. Delta waves produce a deep trance-like state and can enable a person's self-healing processes.

With the help of various methods, you can achieve the most desirable alpha state for daily life, while emphasizing the stimulation of the right brain so you eventually achieve an integration between the two halves of the brain. Ways of doing this include relaxation and yoga exercises, meditational drawing, making mandalas, listening to soft and relaxing music, guided visualizations, as well as memory training, training the (inner) senses, and so on. In all of these activities, singing bowls—either played live or on a CD—can play a helpful role.

Of course, it is also possible to experiment with singing bowls of varying pitches without using these methods. If you have access to equipment such as the electroencephalogram, a mind mirror, or a biofeedback system, you can find out which brain waves occur when you do, think, feel, see, smell or hear, particular things.

With exercise, you can make alpha waves in particular more prevalent, when confronted with situations which would have been stressful in the past, such as examinations or busy traffic, so you can be more relaxed in these situations.

The sound therapist, Hans de Back, recently conducted an experiment in which a number of participants reached a relaxed state with a singing bowl massage within twenty minutes after having visited a busy stock exchange. Equipment was used to measure their brain waves. All the participants achieved the theta level, and more than half included peaks into the delta level.

At the moment, there is still very little known about the real therapeutic value of singing bowls in connection with brain waves. However, in the near future, more and more therapists will experiment with them and use measurement equipment to investigate which brain waves are affected by singing bowls and what other effects there are, although it should not be forgotten that this clinical approach could influence the results.

Aura and Chakra Healing

Many singing bowl therapists perform aura and/or chakra treatments. The aura is the ethereal field that surrounds and penetrates objects and living beings, and can be perceived by sensitive and clairvoyant people as a colored haze. Our physical body and the subtle bodies of the aura (the emotional, mental, astral, spiritual, and ethereal bodies) are inextricably linked and are actually intermingled. The vibrations of music in general, of the planets, colors, and the vibrations of singing bowls are caught by the ethereal body, screened, and passed on to the other bodies. As the ethereal body is the "outer-most" of all these bodies, it works as a sort of shield against negative influences. When tears, dark spots, and holes appear in the ethereal body as the result of stress, worry, violence, or violent emotions, you can no longer function adequately and are psychologically and physically out of balance. A sensitive singing bowl therapist will intuitively hear, see, and/or feel whether there are any weak spots in the aura, and if so, where they are. It is a matter of experimenting, in combination with a high degree of intuition, to find the "correct" tone or the "correct" singing bowl for a particular person's specific complaint.

The most important chakras are wheel-shaped energy centers at the level of the endocrine glands, which form connections between the physical body and cosmic energy passing through the aura. The chakras also correspond to a number of important acupuncture points. Every chakra is linked to a particular color, element, tone, a number of precious stones, and various stages of spiritual consciousness. The chakras play an important role in physical and psychological health.

The Chakra at the Base of the Spine

The chakra at the base of the spine, also known as the base or root chakra, corresponds to the earth element and is connected to the adrenal glands. The corresponding color is red, and the tone is C. The precious stones that correspond to this chakra include: hematite, red jasper, and ruby.

This chakra accommodates the need for security, survival, a feeling of being rooted, grounded, and an awareness of the body. If it is blocked, this can lead, for example, to constipation, sciatica and corpulence.

Sacral Chakra

The sacral chakra is related to the male and female reproductive glands: the testicles and the ovaries. The element is water, the color orange, and the corresponding tone is D. The following precious stones correspond with this chakra: carnelian, fiery opal, and moonstone.

The sacral chakra is responsible for sexuality, wanting to belong to a group, and being able to relate to others. If it is blocked, this can lead to problems with the lower back, the kidneys, the womb, the bladder, and impotence or frigidity.

Solar Plexus

The solar plexus or plexus solaris symbolizes the fire element, and is connected to the pancreas and adrenal glands. The color is yellow and the corresponding tone is E. The precious stones that correspond to this chakra include: amber, citrine and golden topaz.

This chakra accommodates self-confidence, power and energy, as well as the deeper emotions. If the solar plexus is blocked, this can lead to problems such as diabetes, hypoglycemia, and stomach disorders.

Heart Chakra

The heart chakra is connected with the thymus and the element air. The corresponding color is green, and the tone is F. The following precious stones correspond to this chakra: emerald, chrysolite, and aventurine.

This is the chakra of unconditional love, compassion, and the free will of the self. If it is blocked, this can lead to heart and lung disorders, and high blood pressure.

Throat Chakra

The element of the throat chakra is ether, and the related endocrine glands are the thyroid and the hypothalamus. This chakra corresponds to the color blue and the tone G. The corresponding precious stones are: aquamarine, turquoise and lapis lazuli.

This chakra is responsible for creativity, singing, speaking, and inner hearing. If it is blocked this could lead to hearing problems, a stiff neck and shoulders, thyroid disorders (problematic metabolism), and pain in the arms and hands.

Forehead Chakra

The forehead chakra is related to the pineal gland and, therefore, with the element of light or spirit. The color is indigo and the corresponding tone is A. Some of the corresponding precious stones include azurite, lapis lazuli and blue sapphire.

In addition, the third eye is located here; it is the chakra of clairvoyance, intuition, and introspection. If it is blocked, this can lead to visual problems and headaches.

Crown Chakra

The crown chakra is situated at the top of the head and is connected with the element of cosmic consciousness or infinity. The corre-

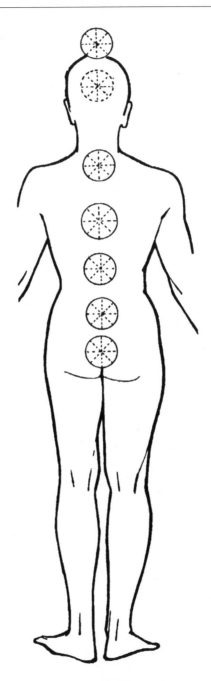

The seven chakras

sponding endocrine gland is the pituitary gland, the tone is B, and the colors associated with this chakra are violet or white. The corresponding stones are: amethyst and fluorspar.

Through the crown chakra you can contact mystical, cosmic elements, and achieve enlightenment, non-duality and ecstasy. If it is blocked, this can result in spiritual or mental confusion, depression, or apathy.

The chakras' relation to particular color frequencies can be perceived intuitively, or clairvoyantly. Many alternative therapies make liberal use of color healing and color visualization to help people restore inner harmony. The need for a particular color or tone can vary at different times. We change, and therefore this need also changes. In fact, every need applies only at a particular time. Chapter 4 devoted some attention to the symbolism of the different colors.

Although the ears obviously perceive sound and resonate with these vibrations—and, as we now know, the cells of the body also absorb these vibrations—we can also perceive sound harmonies, colors, and pitches with the chakras. All these vibrations pass into the spinal cord through the chakras. The vertebrae absorb the vibrations and can direct their resonance to every part of the body along the nervous system, because of their resonance. The body is also able to send the vibrations back to the source of the sound, like a singing bowl or tuning fork. For example, if a singing bowl is resonated and moved along someone's spine from the feet to the head, there may be changes in the sound when the bowl's vibrations come into contact with places where body energy is blocked. These places need treatment and they can be unblocked with the same bowl and pitch, through the interaction between the resonating frequencies of the sound and the chakra. An aura and/or chakra treatment, as well as your own thoughts and feelings, are influenced by the sound in such a way that others can see the color changes in your aura and chakras.

The chakras vibrate at a different frequency in every person, and to some extent it depends on the openness and development of a chakra, and to what extent it is able to transform the vibrations. Furthermore, every singing bowl has such a large range of harmonics that you cannot say that one singing bowl works only on a particular chakra. In principle, every metal singing bowl can be used for every chakra regardless of the timbre or sound, although, generally, bowls with a deep, low sound are used more often for the lower chakras while high, bright sounds are used for the upper body chakras. However, the intuition and intention of the therapist also plays an important role. In this therapy, only metal singing bowls are used, not the crystal singing bowls. A singing bowl can help a chakra to vibrate at the "correct" frequency. You can experiment with this yourself by seeing which color—corresponding to a particular chakra—you perceive when you hear a particular singing bowl.

Chakras and Tones

A study by the didgeridoo healer Jim Wafer shows that the tones C, D, E, F, G, A, and B do not always correspond to the chakras from one to seven in everyone, as described in some books. For most people, C does not have any effect on the chakra at the base of the spine, but D almost always resonates with the sacral chakra. Furthermore, D is a powerful tone for helping to remove blocks in the emotional body.

The tone E works on the solar plexus. The heart chakra is only slightly influenced by F, while A is almost always successful here. The tone G has some influence on the throat chakra, and the forehead chakra is almost always stimulated by A. The crown chakra responds to different tones at different times.

Jim Wafer also conducted experiments with Kirlian photography, with which it is possible to record the energy field surrounding a person. He reports the difference of the hand's energy field hand before and after a digeridoo treatment. In the first photograph in his book, *Vibrational Healing with the Australian Aboriginal Digeridoo,* several "holes" are apparent in places that correspond to different acupuncture meridians. After playing the didgeridoo for half an hour, a second photograph was taken, and this shows that the holes have become smaller, while the energy field around the hand has become larger. In his book, Jim Wafer also explores in greater depth how the balance of energy in the acupuncture points and meridians is restored, in this case with a didgeridoo, but his findings correspond to those of Hans Cousto, which he describes in his book, *The Cosmic Octave*. Cousto describes a number of acupuncture points on various meridians, some of which some correspond to certain chakras, which can be stimulated and restored to equilibrium with the sound of tuning forks with different pitches.

Singing Bowls and Crystals

A number of singing bowl therapists make use of the transforming energy of certain gemstones and crystals, each of which have a unique healing effect corresponding to particular chakras. In gemstone therapy, crystals—especially the Herkimer diamond, as well as tourmaline—have an important place because of their piezoelectrical effect, which is the potential to convert sound vibration into healing energy through an electromagnetic field. Each of these crystal forms has a unique vibration with a basic tone and harmonics, which is known as its "natural" vibration. When the frequency of a sound corresponds to the crystal's natural vibration, there is a resonance that amplifies the vibrations. The sound waves that are created in the crystal are ultrasonic, which means that they are above the audible range. The resulting harmonics are therefore at a high level and their frequencies penetrate the environment or the organs and the cells of the body.

Mountain crystal affects all the chakras and has a supportive and beneficial effect on other stones. You can examine the effects of certain stones on the various chakras in combination with singing bowl vibrations. You can also try to see whether or not singing bowls that produce a strange, "floating sound," in addition to the usual vibration, will produce a more harmonious sound if you place some pieces of crystal or tourmaline around them. The stones neutralize the vibrations and the sound of the bowls become more pleasant to the ear.

In addition to aura/chakra healing and therapy with precious stones, there are a number of other alternative methods related to

Deep relaxation during gong meditation.

vibrations and frequencies that have an influence on the body, mind, and soul. Some of these include aromatherapy, Bach flower remedies, gemstone elixirs, Reiki, Touch for Health, acupuncture, pendulums, color therapy, Aura–Soma therapy, homeopathy, etc. These methods can be successfully combined with singing bowls.

In my opinion, the field is wide-open for far-reaching research into the relationship between the aura, chakras, acupuncture points, precious stones, singing bowls, and the various alternative healing modalities.

Singing Bowls as a Support for Relaxation, Meditation, Concentration, and Transformation

The vibrations of singing bowls can be affect you at the very depth of your soul. Your feelings start to flow in unanticipated directions, forming channels for future events. The timbre of the bowl and the rhythm of the sounds can also bring about unexpected inner transformation.

Most people experience the vibrations of singing bowls as very restful, which is why singing bowls are widely used for relaxation exercises and meditation groups. For treatment, concerts, and workshops with singing bowls, it is essential for the participants to be in or reach a calm and relaxed mood. Only when you are fully relaxed can you surrender and connect with a sound vibration. If you are too tense and shut yourself off from the sounds, the vibrations will actually produce a very unpleasant feeling.

By listening to singing bowls and feeling their vibrations you will be able to work on your own spiritual consciousness. The musical aspect of the bowls becomes sacred activity, particularly when their healing and transforming energies take their effect on you, helping you open the gateway to the unforeseen and mystical life. With quiet and calming sound vibrations, you can experience your own inner beauty, reaching a feeling of joy and satisfaction in this meditative atmosphere.

Perceptions and Eidetic Images

Because your brain starts to produce more alpha and theta waves when you are relaxed, you experience a change of consciousness, a state between sleeping and waking, while remaining aware of your environment. In this state you can have various perceptions, such as sensations on the skin or warmth flowing through the body, as well as seeing colors and/or images. These images can assume all sorts of abstract forms: geometric figures, symbols, mandalas, or snake-like undulations. Realistic images of people and situations may also appear (eidetic images). One participant in a workshop described, "I entered a galactic space without boundaries, in which pulsing points of light floated by from out of the darkness, each with infinite rays of cosmic colors. I floated along on a stream of ethereal light like a sort of Milky Way. I was accompanied by spherical creatures of light. Yes, I am the Sun and they are my planets. Whenever I hear a new sound, another planet is born. I recognize these as the different aspects of my own being; I support them and cherish them. I am open to them and I feel my essence becoming more and more complete." In this alpha-theta state, you sometimes have the feeling that your spirit is empty while you are conscious of it. You are clear, dreamless, sleepless, and without any ideas in your head. This can last a while, followed by a quiet emptiness. In the various forms of Tibetan Buddhist meditation, emptying the mind is the ultimate goal, the achievement of Samadhi. However, Buddhists do not ascribe any value to the forms and images that appear in this way (in contrast to visualizations that are consciously evoked), as they are convinced these are based merely on illusion. Therefore, if images appear, you do not have to connect with them. As they appear, they will also disappear. Try not to force yourself to see images, but listen in an open way, surrender to the sounds, and above all, do not be disappointed if you do not see anything.

Creative Visualizations, Guided Meditations, Fairy Tales and Stories

Several esoteric schools such as shamanism, the Cabbala, Wicca, as well as Tibetan Buddhism, focus on creative visualization, or the conscious creation of mental images in a symbolic story or scheme. A therapist or someone using singing bowls for treatment can also playfully act as an antenna for his clients, carefully bringing them into contact with the real problem with a guided exercise of the imagination or creative visualization. The singing bowl plays a supporting role in bringing people into the right state of consciousness for this activity. The singing bowl is also an excellent accompanying instrument for stories and fairy tales. Just as the ancient Celtic bard strengthened the effect of his poem or story with a harp and the medieval troubadour used the lyre to emphasize certain dramatic moments, a modern storyteller can use singing bowls to create a particular atmosphere and a more lively feeling in a story, fairy tale, or

---

Exercise 11: Combining Singing Bowls with Stories and Poems

An existing story or a story you have written yourself, a fairy tale, poem, or a mantra or prayer can be accompanied by the sounds of singing bowls.

Place two or three singing bowls in front of you, each with a pitch that you enjoy. As you read, declaim, or recite, strike the singing bowl with a wooden beater or stick when you come upon the words you want to stress, depending on whether you want to achieve a stimulating or calming effect.

---

guided meditation.

At the beginning and end of a story or meditation/visualization exercise, the storyteller produces a low, dark sound (and sometimes adds bright tingshas with a higher tone) at a restful moment, to indicate the beginning and end, and to bring him or herself and the group in tune with each other. Dark sounds will have a relaxing and meditational effect in a story while higher, bright sounds create an alert and exciting atmosphere. This can also apply to using of singing bowls with shaman dream journeys or astral journeys.

Singing Bowl Concerts; the Singing Bowl as an Accompanying Instrument

When musicians give a live performance with singing bowls, it is

---

Exercise 12: Group Improvisation

Everyone should have their favorite singing bowl with them and impro-
vise together, creating a sound composition from nothingness. You will be
astonished to see how harmonious this can sound. You can also have a
jam session with several different instruments that go together well with
singing bowls.

---

important for them to be in contact with their public during the
concert. If there is a good and serene interaction, the chances are
that there will be a unique sense of cosmic unity between them. In
a concert with a small audience or during workshops or group sessions, it can be a very special experience when everyone brings his
or her own singing bowl and plays it.

In addition to the personal enjoyment you can feel from experimenting with sound, improvising and experiencing rhythms with a
group of people can evoke a sacred resonance in the group and
unleash primal feelings. As Dries Langeveld once remarked, "It happens of its own accord, through you."

There are singing bowl concerts in which only the bronze bowls
are featured, but of course there are also concerts with several
instruments such as drums, gongs, cymbals, tingshas, Tibetan bells,
yak horns, didgeridoos, pan pipes, kalimbas (thumb piano), xylo-
phones, etc., which may also be combined with vocal harmonics
and/or mantras. A musician playing singing bowls on his own is
obviously more limited in his choice of instruments than when he's
with a group of musicians. In recordings, sophisticated techniques
and sound mixers can reproduce an large orchestra of singing bowls
played by just one person.

The music of singing bowls, both played live and recorded on
CD, is eminently suitable for accompanying several different activities: for rituals and ceremonies, for dance and movement, tai chi
and chi kung, yoga, massage, and all sorts of creative and meditative
therapies. In short, there is an infinite range of possibilities for work-

ing with singing bowls.

Other Applications for Singing Bowls

I previously discussed, working with singing bowls in physical and psychological heath care. However, this is still at an early, experimental stage. Nevertheless, it is possible to say that it is quite clear that the vibrations of singing bowls have a positive influence on a sense of well-being in general. They can:

- stimulate life energy;
- foster rest and relaxation;
- help relieve insomnia;
- improve concentration;
- normalize blood pressure;
- restore the equilibrium of the immune system;
- synchronize the left and right hemispheres of the brain;
- increase creativity;
- improve the sense of hearing;
- harmonize respiration;
- put people at ease.

All in all, this is a whole series of effects that contribute to an increase in the joy of life and general vitality, enabling us to deal with complaints provoked by a state of imbalance. Singing bowls help us find relief from all sorts of psychosomatic complaints and illnesses, such as headache, migraine, high blood pressure, asthma, allergies, bedwetting, stuttering, back complaints, etc.

Singing Bowls Are not an Alternative to Medicine!

However, the vibrations of singing bowls cannot take the place of medication that may need to be prescribed by a doctor. Therefore, in the case of persistent complaints, chronic or serious diseases such as cancer, AIDS, heart conditions, psychiatric illnesses, etc., it is always important to consult a doctor before giving or receiving any treatment with singing bowls.

The Music of the Future
The possibilities for the further application of healing practices with singing bowls exist in the following areas, where experiments are already being conducted on a small scale and will undoubtedly in the future become more wide-ranging:

- during pregnancy, beginning in the fourth month;
- for babies in incubators and restless babies and toddlers;
- the mentally handicapped and autistic patients;
- patients with Alzheimer's disease;
- comatose patients and the terminally ill;
- other possible applications yet to be discovered!

Healing with singing bowls is still in its infancy. The methods, exercises, and other applications presented here are largely based on ancient shamanic healing techniques from various cultures, supplemented with insights from modern psychology, general sound and music therapy and different alternative healing methods. Therefore these applied methods and techniques are not a replacement for classical medicine but should be seen as a guideline and a signpost toward consciousness, healing, and transformation for anyone who is searching for his or her true essence.

Tuned

to the primal sound

of Life

the veils disappear

—Annema Raven

Bibliography

Andrews, Ted. *Crystal Balls & Crystal Bowls: Tools for Ancient Scrying & Modern Seership.* St. Paul: Llewellyn Publications, 1995.

————. Sacred Sounds: *Transformation through Music & Word.* St. Paul: Llewellyn Publications, 1992.

Beaulieu, John. *Music and Sound in the Healing Arts: An Engergy Approach.* Quasha, George, ed. Barrytown, NY: Station Hill Press, 1987.

Beesley, Ronald P. *The Robe of Many Colors.* Speldhurst, Kent: White Lodge Publishing, 1970.

Berendt, Joachim-Ernst. *Ik hoor dus ik ben: Werkboek & leerboek over de kunst van het luisteren.* Katwijk aan Zee, Holland: Panta Rhei, 1990.

Berendt, Joachim and Frithof Capra. Nada Brahma: *The World is Sound.* Capra, Frithof, ed. Rochester, VT: Inner Traditions, 1987.

Connell, Monica. *Against a Peacock Sky.* London: Viking, 1991.

Cornu, Philippe. *Tibetan Astrology.* Boston & London: Shambhala, 1997.

Cousto, Hans. *The Cosmic Octave.* Mendocino: LifeRhythm, 1988.

Dewhurst-Maddock, Olivea. *The Book of Sound Therapy: Heal Yourself with Music & Voice.* New York: Simon & Schuster, 1993.

Dijk-Karanika, Katerina van. "Ziekte en de vijf dimensies van het menselijk bestaan." *Tijdschrift Bres,* Vol. 171. Amsterdam: Bres, 1995.

Hamaker-Zondag, Karen. *Planetary Symbolism in the Horoscope.* York Beach, Maine: Samuel Weiser, 1985.

Huibers, Jaap. *Gezond zijn met Metalen.* Deventer, Holland: Ankh-Hermes, 1981.

Jansen, Eva Rudy. *Singing Bowls: A Practical Handbook of Instruction and Use.* Havelte, Holland: Binkey Kok Publications, 1990.

Judith, Anodea. *Wheeles of Life: A User's Guide to the Chakra System.* St. Paul: Llewellyn Publications, 1987.

Julius, F.H. *Klank tussen stof en geest.* Zevenster: Zeist, 1983.

Kaste, Christian de. "Klankschalen en Muziektherapie." *Tijdschrift Bres,* Vol. 191, Amsterdam: Bres, 1998.

Khan, Inayat. *Music.* Surrey: Farnham, 1962.

————. *Music of Life.* New Lebanon, NY: Omega Publications, 1991.

————. *Mysticism of Sound.* Pomeroy, WA: Health Research, 1972.

————. *The Mysticism of Sound & Music.* New Lebanon, NY: Omega Publications, 1991.

Langedijk, Pieter. *Alpha-hersengolven.* Deventer, Holland: Ankh-Hermes, 1989.

Langeveld, Dries. "Het raadsel van de zingende schalen: Een reconstructie van herkomst en gebruik." *Tijdschrift Bres,* Vol. 120. Amsterdam: Bres, 1986.

Müller, Else. *Der Klang der Bilder: Phantasiereisen mit Klangschalen.* Munich: Kösel Verlag, 1996.

Pelikan, Wilhelm. *Sieben Metalle.* Dornach, Switzerland: Verlag am Goetheanum, 1996.

Purce, Jill. "De helende kracht van geluid." *Tijdschrift Bres,* Vol. 120. Amsterdam: Bres, 1986.

Soos, Joska. *Ik genees niet, ik herstel de energie.* Amsterdam: Karnak, 1985.

Verbeke, Geert. *Klankschalen Klinken.* Papendrecht: Crystal Vision, 1997.

Wafer, Jim. *Vibrational Healing with the Australian Aboriginal Didgeridoo.* Crystal Lake, IL: Jim Wafer, n.d.

Discography

Back, Hans de. *A Gentle Touch of Sound*. NVG CD 02894, n.d.
———. *Gong Meditation*. Havelte: Binkey Kok, 1992
———. *Hans de Back in Concert*. 1991.
———. *Singing Bowl Chakra Meditation*. Havelte: Binkey Kok, 1992.
Becher, Danny and Fred Vogels. *Floating Spirits and the Dancing Universe: Meditative Music on Singing Bowls from Nepal, Tibet, Japan and Thailand*. Zutphen: Danny Becher, 1987.
———. *Natural: Transformation through the Healing Qualities of Sound*. Aerdenhout: Oreade, 1992.
Berendt, Joachim-Ernst. *Primordial Tones 1: The Tones of the Earth, the Sun, the Moon, and the Shiva-Shakti Sound*. Rochester, VT: Destiny Recordings, 1994.
———. *Urtöne 2: Die Töne des Mars, der Venus, des Jupiters, der Karuna-Klang*. Freiburg: Verlag Hermann Bauer, n.d.
———. *Urtöne 3: Die Töne von Saturn, Merkur, Uranus, Neptun, Pluto und der Kosmische Zusammenklang Sämtlicher Himmelskörper unseres Planetensystems*. Freiburg: Verlag Hermann Bauer, 1990.
Ingerman, Sandra. *Tibetan Bowl Sound for the Shamanic Journey: Shamanic Journey Series, No. 4*. Mill Valley, CA: Foundation for Shamanic Studies, 1988.
Langeveld, Dries. *Savage Silence: On Himalayan Bowls*. Amsterdam: Keyton, 1996.
Precencer, Alan. *The Singing Bowls of Tibet: Mysterious & Ancient Sounds from Singing Bowls, Conch & Yak Horns, Gongs & Cymbals*. Badminton: Saydisc Records, 1981.
Soos, Joska. Shamanic *Ritual Music I: Kant B: Music of Spheres for the 6th and 7th Chakras*. Amsterdam: Karnak, n.d.
Tillmann, Rainer. *The Purity of Sound: An Acoustic Recording of Singing Bowls for Meditation*. Havelte: Binkey Kok, 1996.
———. *The Sounds of the Planets / 1: Meditations with the Planet Sounds of Tibetan Singing Bowls: Earth Year Tone, Saturn, Venus, Sun*. Havelte: Binkey Kok, 1997.
Weise, Klaus. *Neptune: Tibetan Singing Bowls*. Grafing: Aquamarin Verlag, n.d.

————. *Space*. Grafing, Aquamarin Verlag, n.d. (Note: indirectly, this recording is linked to Saturn's planet tone.)

————. *Tibetische Klangschalen*. Munich: Edition Akasha, 1990.

————. *Uranus: Tibetan Singing Bowls*. Grafing: Aquamarin Verlag, n.d.

About the Author

Anneke Huyser, born in the heart of Amsterdam, now lives in a village in the northern Netherlands with her husband, youngest daughter, two dogs, and one cat. Her interests cover a wide range of topics, such as transpersonal and Jungian psychology, mandalas, women's spirituality, archeology, and Eastern & Western philosophy.

She and her husband own the metaphysical book store, De Wijze Kater, in Utrecht. She is a well known author of several metaphysical Dutch books on creating personal mandalas, elemental energies, and gemstones.

Since 1995, she has been giving lectures and workshops on creating personal mandalas and about the history and use of singing bowls. She is part of a group of women who are editing a unique, quarterly periodical about mandalas.

Anneke Huyser has translated English and German books about the tarot including, *The Goddess Tarot* by Kriss Waldherr. She has also translated Lao Tzu's *Te-Tao Ching* (edited by Robert G. Hendricks), Stanislav Grof's *Auf der Schwelle zum Leben* and a channeled book by the British healer Ian Graham about the teachings of White Bull, *God is Never Late! (But He's Never Early, Either)*.

CDs and Cassettes from Binkey Kok

Gong Meditation
Hans de Back

Chakra Meditation
Hans de Back

Hans de Back in Concert
Hans de Back

Singing Bowl Meditation
Hans de Back

Didgeridoo
Barramundi

The Purity of Sound
An Acoustic Recording of Singing Bowls for Meditation
Rainer Tillmann

The Sounds of Planets/1
Meditation with the Planet Sounds of Tibetan Singing Bowls
Rainer Tillmann

The Sounds of Planets/2
Meditation with the Planet Sounds of Tibetan Singing Bowls
Rainer Tillmann

Crystal Sounds Deva
Meditation with the pure and harmonic vibrations of Crystal
Singing Bowls
Rainer Tillmann

Soma Sounds for Healing/1
Crystal and Tibetan Singing Bowls for meditation and healing
Rainer Tillmann

Prna Sounds for Healing/2
Gongs and Tibetan Singing Bowls for meditation and healing
Rainer Tillmann

CD sampler
One hour meditation Music with tracks from the above CD's